Sybil Rides

| The True Story of Sybil Ludington
The Female Paul Revere
The Burning of Danbury and Battle of Ridgefield |
|---|

Elementary Reader Edition

By

Larry A. Maxwell

Larry A. Maxwell

Dedicated To
The Young People who are our future heroes.

Cover Designed by Matthew R. Maxwell
Featuring a 13 Star American Flag
And the Sybil Ludington Monument
on Route 52 in Carmel, NY

Sybil Rides

1775 Productions

599 Route 311, Patterson, New York 12563
1130 Perry Rd., Afton, New York 13730
GoodInformation.US

ISBN-13: 978-1-949277-07-4

Creative Non-Fiction

New York History; Connecticut History; History of the American Revolutionary War; Military History; Biographies of Women; Biographies of Adolescents; Biographies of Military History

Reenactors in pictures in this book belong to the Brigade of the American Revolution, Continental Line, British Brigade and/or the Living History Guild.
These organizations help keep history alive.

All illustrations in this book are either in the public domain or used by permission. Photographs by Larry A. Maxwell and Gary Vorwald are copyrighted with this book. All rights reserved.

© COPYRIGHT 2019 – Larry A. Maxwell

Larry A. Maxwell

Table of Contents

Chapter   **Page**

	List of Illustrations	8
	Introduction	11
Chapter 1	Paul Revere's Dangerous Ride	15
Chapter 2	War Begins	23
Chapter 3	Meet Sybil's Family	31
Chapter 4	A Plan to End the War	37
Chapter 5	Enoch Crosby the Spy	49
Chapter 6	The Loyalists Plot	60
Chapter 7	Crosby Warns Ludington	69
Chapter 8	Attempt to Capture Ludington	78
Chapter 9	Conflict at the Ganong's Home	88
Chapter 10	Sybil's Birthday Party	94
Chapter 11	British Fleet Embarks for Norwalk	108
Chapter 12	Shooting Muskets	112
Chapter 13	Crown Forces Land at Norwalk	120
Chapter 14	Conflict Between Father and Son	126
Chapter 15	Confrontation at Bethel	129
Chapter 16	Danbury Attacked	135
Chapter 17	American Officers Meet at Redding	145
Chapter 18	Messenger Arrives at Ludington's	153
Chapter 19	Sybil Arrives at the First House	160
Chapter 20	The Looting and Burning Continue	163
Chapter 21	Sybil and the Bandits	166
Chapter 22	Americans Arrive in Bethel	170
Chapter 23	Sybil Arrives at Another Home	173
Chapter 24	Making Ammunition	176
Chapter 25	Sybil Faces an Obstacle	181
Chapter 26	Militia March off to Battle	184
Chapter 27	Sybil at the Ganong's	189
Chapter 28	Crown Forces Leave Danbury	192
Chapter 29	Sybil Rides as the Sun Rises	196
Chapter 30	American Officers Plan Response	199
Chapter 31	Opposition South of Danbury	203
Chapter 32	Sybil at the Last Home	206
Chapter 33	Wooster Attacks the Crown Forces	209

Chapter 34	Sybil Returns Home	214
Chapter 35	Barricades in Ridgefield	220
Chapter 36	Battle in Ridgefield	223
Chapter 37	Crown Forces South of Ridgefield	233
Chapter 38	Ludington Meets Arnold	239
Chapter 39	Back at the Ludington's Home	247
Chapter 40	British Officers Before Last Battle	250
Chapter 41	Battle in Norwalk	255
Chapter 42	The Smoke Clears	261
Chapter 43	The Return	265
About the Author		271

Sybil Ludington Monument Dedication

Enoch Crosby Chapter of the Daughters of the American Revolution, Along Lake Gleneida, Carmel, New York, 1961.
Photo Courtesy of the Putnam County Historian's Office

List of Illustrations

Illustration	Page
Sybil Ludington Monument	Cover
Sybil Ludington Monument Dedication	7
Royal Naval Ships in Boston Harbor	14
1775 Map of Boston and Surrounding Area	16
Paul Revere Being Rowed to Charlestown	18
H.M.S. Somerset	19
Paul Revere's Ride	22
Battle of Lexington	27
British Regulars Advance on Concord	28
Minutemen Fire on Retreating Regulars	29
Portrait of Sybil Ludington	30
Ludington Mill	32
225th Anniversary of Sybil's Ride	33
1776 British Map of New York City	38
Portrait of The Lord William Howe	40
Portrait of Sir William Erskine	41
Portrait of Governor William Tryon	42
Van Wyck Homestead - Fishkill Supply Depot	44
Colonial Log Church	50
Portrait of Enoch Crosby	56
Drumming Out of Town	61
Inside a Colonial Tavern	63
An Integrated Militia	70
Loyalists Seek to Apprehend Colonel Ludington	79
Colonial Two-Story Home	83
Colonial Bedroom	86
Home of Loyalist Beverley Robinson	89
Hanging of Nathan Hale	92
Rev. John Gano	95
Haym Salomon Silver Medal	96
Sketch of a Stockbridge/Wappinger Indian	99
Daniel Nimham, Sachem of the Wappingers	100
Route the British Fleet Took to Compo Beach	111
Loading a Musket	119
Compo Beach Photographs	121
Crown Forces Landing at Compo Beach	123
Tory Tax Collector	128
Crown Forces Wait for Enemy to Attack	131

1796 German Map of Connecticut	134
Portrait of Colonel Joseph Platt Cooke	137
Musicians Play as Crown Forces Enter Town	138
The Liberty Flag	140
Danbury Raid Monument	144
Portrait of General Benedict Arnold	147
Portrait of General David Wooster	149
Take Notice Recruitment Poster	152
Approximate Route of Sybil's Ride	159
Simple Colonial Home	161
Militiaman Prepares to Respond to the Call	162
Highwaymen Robbing a Traveler	167
Crown Forces Raid and Burn	171
Colonial Home	174
Colonial Militia Respond to the Call	175
Musket Tool	177
Inside a Typical Colonial Home	179
Overflowing Stream in Putnam County	183
Revolutionary War Militiaman on Horse	187
Sybil Rides on Through the Night	189
Crown Forces Leaving Town	193
1777 Map of Tryon's Raid on Danbury	195
Sunrise Over the Hills	197
Colonial Fairfield County Connecticut	200
Colonel Jedediah Huntington	202
Militiamen Attack Crown Forces	204
Loyalists Return Fire	205
Kitchen in a Typical Colonial Home	207
Historical Marker for Sybil's Ride	208
Monument to General David Wooster	213
The Minute-Men of the Revolution	214
Sybil Ludington's Ride Ends	215
Colonial Militia Assemble	217
Militia at the 225th Anniversary of Sybil's Ride	219
Barricade at Ridgefield	221
Battle of Ridgefield	225
Battle of Ridgefield Historic Marker	226
Cannon Crew Fires	228
Cannonball in Keeler Tavern	230
Exploit of Benedict Arnold	231
Soldiers Return Fire Under Cover	233
Continentals Attack from Woods	234

Crown Forces Fall to Militia Attack	235
Continental Artillery Fire Cannon	240
Portrait of Colonel John Lamb	245
Colonial Dining Area	249
Continental Army and Militia on the March	251
Continental Soldiers Maneuvering to Battle	258
Patriot's Monument at Compo Beach	260
The Battle of Compo Hill by Hannan	262
The Battle of Cedar Point by Hannan	262
Friend Helping Wounded Soldier	263
Newspaper Advertisement for Lost British Army	264
Soldiers Return from Battle	267
Tombstones of Sybil and Colonel Henry Ludington	270
Larry A. Maxwell	271

Introduction

Sybil Rides tells the inspiring true story of events during the American Revolution which resulted in sixteen-year old Sybil Ludington becoming known as the *Female Paul Revere*. Her ride took place during an event in American History designed by the British Commanders to bring an end to the Revolutionary War.

On a cold rainy night in the spring of 1777, the British Regular Army, along with some Loyalists, attacked and burned Danbury, Connecticut. That raid was part of Lord William Howe's plan to end the Revolution. During the raid a messenger was sent to the home of Colonel Henry Ludington asking for help. The Colonel's sixteen-year old daughter, Sybil, bravely rode forty miles on that cold rainy night throughout the Hudson Valley to call the Militia to action.

On her ride Sybil stopped quickly at each home, banged on the doors and windows, and yelled, *"Call to arms! The Regulars and Tories are burning Danbury! The Militia is needed! Call to arms!"* Families woke. Men dressed quickly, grabbed their muskets, and headed into the night to face a powerful enemy. Sybil's brave ride earned her the nickname, *The Female Paul Revere*.

A larger than life monument honoring Sybil

Ludington, stands in Carmel, New York along the route where she made her historic ride. It shows her riding on her horse as she rode to call out the Militia.

This story starts at the beginning of the Revolutionary War with Paul Revere in a rowboat in Boston Harbor, two years before Sybil's ride.

From there it goes to Lexington, Massachusetts, where we see the Militia who responded to Revere's call and faced the might of the British Army.

We then watch the war shift to New York.

All events and characters in this book are historical.

This story tells the true story of Sybil Ludington and of her father, Colonel Henry Ludington, his family, and other unsung heroes.

In this book you will meet British officers and their Loyalists allies and see the conflicts between them.

You will see the brave, yet funny way Sybil and her siblings stop the Loyalists attempt to capture their father.

You will meet Enoch Crosby, a friend of the Ludingtons, who served as a spy in the struggle for independence.

You will meet Jacob Angevine, a former slave who earned his freedom and that of his family, by serving in the French and Indian War. You will also meet Joseph, his teenage son, who is a friend of Sybil Ludington and a brave member of the Colonel Ludington's Militia.

You will meet John Gano the famous *Fighting Preacher* and his friend, Haym Salomon, a Jewish immigrant who helped get funding for the Revolution.

You will meet Daniel Nimham, Sachem (chief) of the Wappinger Indians and his son Abraham, true unsung American heroes who sacrificed everything.

You will see how Luther Holcomb, another brave young unsung hero, helped delay the entire British Army and its attack on Danbury.

One of the surprising characters you will meet is Benedict Arnold who later becomes America's most notorious traitor. He was once a hero and played an inspiring important part in this story.

This Elementary Reader Edition was designed for Elementary School Students. It includes all the chapters, events and dialogue as the Regular and Expanded editions. It uses a slightly larger typestyle. The sentence structure and vocabulary are geared to make it a better read for the Elementary student. There are a few more illustrations than in the Regular edition.

Hopefully this book will help bring history alive and inspire you as you read this true story about Sybil Ludington and some unsung American heroes.

Larry A. Maxwell

Royal Naval Ships in Boston Harbor
Drawing by Paul Revere.

Chapter 1

Paul Revere's Dangerous Ride
Boston Harbor
April 18, 1775 – Tuesday Evening

An almost full-moon arose on a cloudy, cold spring night in Boston, Massachusetts. The date was April 18, 1775. Dark dreary clouds filled the chilly air and surrounded the many warships docked in Boston Harbor.

Each ship was filled with British Regulars who huddled together trying to keep warm. They could tell something very important was about to happen.

The British commanders in Boston planned to send a large force of Regulars to Lexington, Massachusetts, to arrest Samuel Adams and John Hancock, leaders of the *Sons of Liberty*. The plan was an attempt to end what they feared could be a possible revolution. Instead of preventing a revolution they were about to start one.

About 9:30 p.m. a local silversmith, who was one of the *Sons of Liberty*, closed his shop and tried to leave the city without being noticed. He quietly headed up the street toward the harbor. He had to be careful because the British Military leaders expected trouble and posted British Regular soldiers all around town. Anyone out on the street that night would be arrested.

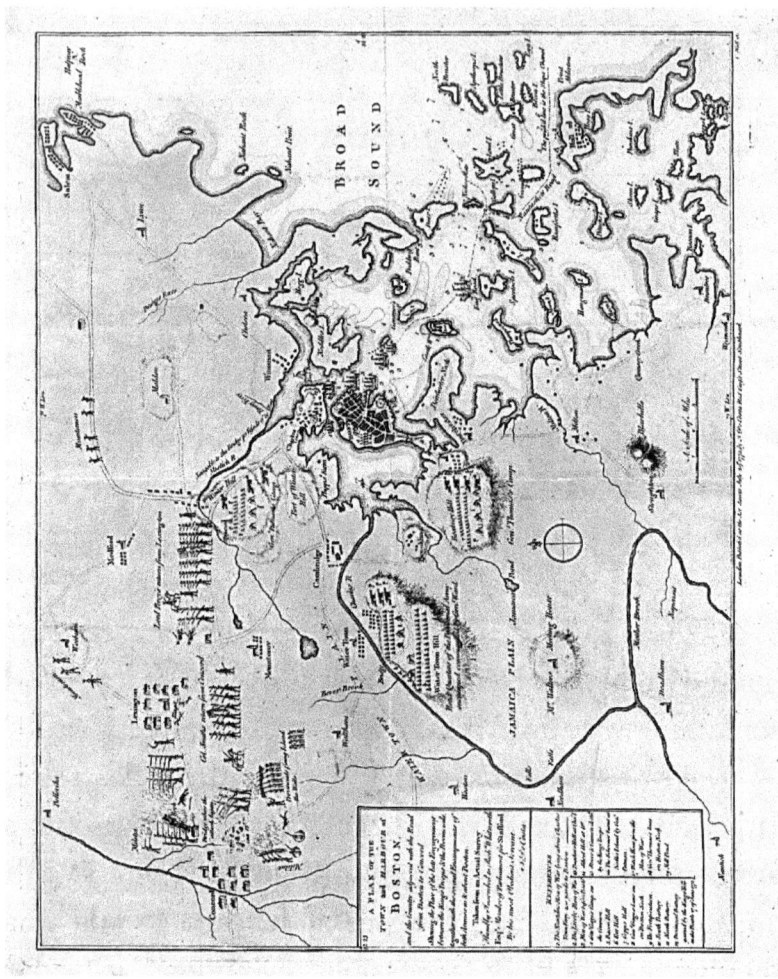

1775 Map of Boston and Surrounding Area

By J. DeCosta, Published in London, 1775.

The silversmith proceeded quietly through Boston streets. He finally made it to the docks. There he saw the Regulars boarding war ships.

He looked for two men with a small rowboat. They were to take him across the Charles River to Charlestown.

Suddenly he heard footsteps and slipped back into the shadows. The sound of the footsteps grew louder and louder. He held his breath and leaned closer to the building trying to disappear.

A large dark figure approached. He strained his eyes to see if it was wearing a military uniform. When he saw the man was dressed in workman's clothes he breathed a big sigh of relief. It was his shipbuilder friend, Joshua Bentley.

Joshua quietly asked, "Paul Revere, is that you?"

He replied, "Yes, it is I. And I am so glad to see you, Joshua."

They shook hands. Then Joshua motioned for Paul Revere to follow him. "Come this way Paul, Thomas Richardson is waiting for us in the rowboat."

The two men walked quickly and quietly to the rowboat, carefully looking around, doing their best to make sure they were not discovered.

Joshua spoke with concern to Paul Revere, "There has been a lot of activity around here. I hope we can get you across the river in time to warn Adams and Hancock."

They walked down the dock and arrived at a large rowboat. Thomas Richardson was waiting next to the rowboat, holding a set of oars.

As Joshua stepped into the rowboat, Thomas greeted Paul Revere, "Paul it is good to see you."

As Paul Revere entered the boat, Thomas said, "I hope you do not get seasick."

Paul Revere responded, "I will gladly take sea

sickness over being spotted and shot by a musket from a British war ship."

They pushed off from the dock and began to quietly row across the Charles River.

Paul Revere Being Rowed to Charlestown
By A. Lassell Ripley.
Paul Revere Memorial Association

The river was filled with British war ships. On each ship, were British Regulars dressed in red wool coats. They huddled in groups trying to keep warm on that cold chilly night. They were glad they brought black woolen blankets.

Joshua and Thomas worked hard to row the boat,. They tried to be as quiet as possible, so they would not be discovered. That was not an easy task.

As they came close to the H.M.S. Somerset, a British Warship, Paul Revere hoped no one would see them. He softly said to the others, "Try to be extra quiet. We must not let the sentries discover us."

H.M.S. Somerset
18th Century Engraving.

Joshua quietly replied. "We are doing our best."

Paul Revere spoke again, with concern, "Lives depend on us."

Thomas whispered, "I imagine it will be our lives, if we are caught!"

Once they rowed safely past the ship, Joshua was relieved. He whispered, "That was close."

"That was very close," Paul Revere said, "Well done!"

As they rowed further away, Paul Revere looked toward the shore and said, "If we can find Deacon Larkin, and if he has a horse ready for me, I should be able to reach Lexington in time to warn Adams and Hancock."

Deacon John Larkin, a member of the Sons of Liberty, was waiting along the shore. He was also looking for a signal from the Church.

If the Sons of Liberty discovered the Regulars planned to attack by land, they would place one lantern in the steeple of the North Church. If the attack would come by sea, it would be two lanterns.

As he waited, Deacon Larkin saw two lanterns. He knew the attack would come by sea.

When the rowboat landed, Paul Revere looked up and down the shore and saw his friend. Deacon Larkin was standing near the shore with a horse.

As Paul Revere stepped out of the boat he turned to Thomas and Joshua and said, "Thank you so much for rowing me across, you will probably be unsung heroes in the story which is about to unfold."

Joshua and Thomas tipped their hats. Joshua proudly said, "We are willing to do anything for the sake of liberty!

Paul Revere came up to Deacon John Larkin. As they warmly shook hands Deacon Larkin said, "Paul Revere! I am glad you made it."

Paul Revere responded, "Deacon John Larkin! I am so glad to see you too."

Deacon Larkin's tone quickly changed to concern,

"Paul, there are more sentries and patrols out tonight, than I have seen in weeks."

Paul Revere agreed, yet said, "John, that is because, the time has come."

He then said, "We received definite word from sources close to General Gage. The Regulars are heading out in force, in the morning, to try to arrest Samuel Adams and John Hancock at Lexington and to confiscate our muskets and cannons at Concord."

Deacon Larkin said, "I am sure they would love to capture the leaders of the Sons of Liberty. That would be a serious blow to our cause."

Deacon Larkin turned toward the horse he brought and offered the reins to Paul Revere. "I have this horse all saddled and ready for you, just as you requested."

Paul Revere said, "William Dawes set out earlier on his horse, across Boston Neck for Lexington. I must also head to Lexington. We are expecting opposition along the way. With God's help, by taking two different routes, one of us is sure to make it."

Deacon Larkin helped steady the horse as Paul Revere stepped up and sat in the saddle. Then he said, "The other riders have been ready for days to head out and summon the Militia from surrounding towns and villages. We have been waiting for your arrival and for news to see if the Regulars would be coming by land or sea. I will let the other riders know the Regulars are coming by sea, and they will ride and let the others know the time has come to take a stand."

The horse moved about. Paul Revere pulled on the reins and said, "I must be on my way to call out the Militia and to warn Adams and Hancock!"

As he then rode off, Deacon Larkin shouted, "God speed!"

Paul Revere galloped off down the road and shouted, "The Regulars are coming! The Regulars are coming!"

Paul Revere's Ride

Engraving by Charles Green Bush (1842-1909).
New York Public Library

Chapter 2

War Begins

Lexington
April 19, 1775 – Early Wednesday Morning

It was about one-thirty in the morning, on April 19, 1775, when Paul Revere and William Dawes rode into in Lexington, Massachusetts. They let people know the Regulars were coming.

Captain John Parker, head of the Lexington Training Band ordered bell rung to call the Militia. Men rose from their beds, grabbed their muskets, and quickly came to the town green.

Hearts were beating like drums. Everyone waited for the arrival of the British Regulars. They were told to stay in line and let the Regulars pass by.

Scouts were sent to find out how long it would be until the Regulars arrived. They returned and told Captain Parker the Regulars were a few hours away. He allowed some men to go back to their homes to get some rest. Some waited at John Buckman's tavern.

At about four-fifteen in the morning, Thaddeus Bowman, one of the scouts, returned after he saw the

Regulars coming on the road from Boston. Captain Parker had the drummer play to call the Militia.

As quickly as they could, all the men in the Lexington Training Band came to the town green. Captain Parker had them line up on the right side, parallel to the road.

British Light Infantry were coming quickly down the road, toward Lexington. They were led by forty-four-year-old British Marine Lieutenant Jesse Adair. He was riding on horseback.

Lieutenant Adair and his men made the long all-night march from Cambridge to Lexington. Two days of rain made the roads muddy and streams run high. That made the march harder.

They were coming to arrest Samuel Adams and John Hancock, two leaders of the Sons of Liberty.

Adair was angry the way people in Boston mistreated him and his men. His men were cursed at and even spit upon. They wanted to put an end to this conflict.

The Militia was more prepared than the Regulars knew. Each town had its own Militia. They drilled regularly to defend their town from danger.

Though all the members of the Lexington Training Band trained regularly. Most had never been in a battle, nor fired a musket at another person. The ones who had been in battle had not done it since the war with the French and Indians. That war ended twelve years ago. Now the army, which they once fought next to, were sent to fight against them. That gave them a strange feeling.

Some seventy men waited with Captain Parker, on

one side of the Lexington town green. They had their muskets in their hands.

Parker looked across the bridge, and down the road. Finally, he saw a large force of Regulars coming down the road, led by a British officer on horseback.

Parker shouted, "Here they come! Form a line!"

The men quickly formed a line next to the road. They lined up in a way to not block the Regulars from passing. Parker hoped the Crown would peacefully pass through.

Parker prepared his men for a possible fight. He yelled out the command, "Prime and load!"

Each man quickly loaded their muskets.

Lieutenant Adair arrived on horseback with the Regulars behind him. When they were about thirty yards away, he pulled out his sword. He held it up above his head and shouted, "From column into line!"

The Regulars formed two rows, facing the Militia.

Fear filled the hearts of the Militia when Adair yelled to his men the command, "Prime and load!"

The Regulars loaded their guns. Then they stood with muskets held in front of their faces, waiting for the command to *Fire*.

Both groups were loaded, facing each other.

Parker's men fearfully looked across the field at the Regulars, who clearly outnumbered them.

Lieutenant Adair waved his sword in the air. He shouted "Huzzah!" Hoping to scare the Rebels.

His men shouted out, "Huzzah! Huzzah! Huzzah!"

Captain Parker and his men were scared but held

their position.

Then, suddenly the ground rumbled as Major John Pitcairn, Lieutenant Adair's superior officer, came riding at a gallop to the front line. He waved his pistol in the air. More soldiers followed him. We he came to the front he took command.

Major Pitcairn waved his pistol in the air, signaling the Regulars to stop shouting. They quickly stopped.

Pitcairn was angry to see the Militia loaded and standing with muskets, across from his men. He yelled, "Throw down your arms! You damned Rebels, or you are all dead men!"

Some Militia looked at each other in fear.

Captain Parker saw their fear. He yelled to his men, "Stand your ground!"

His courage made those who looked ready to run, stand firm. They held their muskets tighter and bravely faced the Regulars.

Parker then yelled again to his men, "Do not fire!"

He paused for a moment.

After hearing Parker's words, Major Pitcairn thought he stopped the Rebels. He nodded his head to Lieutenant Adair with a big smile on his face.

That smile quickly disappeared when he heard Parker continue and say "... Unless fired upon!"

Pitcairn was very angry.

Parker looked back at him and yelled to his men, "If they want a war, let it begin here!"

Each side quietly and fearfully looked at the other.

Suddenly, the quiet was broken a Boom! It was the loud blast of a single musket.

It was not clear where that shot came from. It became known as, *the shot heard round the world.*

Battle of Lexington, April 19, 1775

By John H. Daniels & Sons, Boston, printed 1903.
Library of Congress, Washington, D.C.

That first shot did not hit anyone. After a very brief pause a few of the Militia fired their muskets. Then, afraid that they were being fired upon by the Regulars, all the Militia fired their muskets.

One of the Regulars was hit. Major Pitcairn's horse was struck twice.

When Lieutenant Adair saw Pitcairn's horse was hit, he yelled to his men, "Make Ready! Present! Fire!"

The ground shook as the Regulars fired. Bullets flew across the field, hitting some Militia.

After that deadly blow, Captain Parker yelled to his

men, "Fall back! Take care of yourself!"

Many went behind a stone wall looking for cover.

Adair commanded the Regulars, "Fix, bayonets!"

They put their bayonets on the end of their muskets.

Adair then gave the command, "Advance!"

The Regulars pointed their muskets at the Rebels and marched across the field yelling, "Huzzah!" Their bayonets gleamed in the morning sun. The Militia quickly fled.

The Regulars were about to enter the homes of the Militia and take what they wanted. They stopped when they heard the drums calling them to line up.

British Regulars Advance on Concord

*By Amos Doolittle (1754-1832).
Doolittle visited battlefields and interviewed survivors*

Major Pitcairn ended the conflict by leading his men to Concord, hoping to destroy the Rebel's guns. They were attacked at Concord by two hundred and fifty Militia. They outnumbered the Militia and drove them away.

The Regulars searched Concord for Rebel leaders and supplies and could not find them.

As the Regulars marched back to Boston, hundreds of Militia fired upon them from behind stone walls and trees. Many were killed or wounded.

Lieutenant Jesse Adair survived the war. Major John Pitcairn died less than two months later at the Battle of Bunker Hill.

Minutemen Fire on Retreating Regulars
Engraving 1800's.

Larry A. Maxwell

Historically Accurate Portrait of Sybil Ludington

This image by Hal Bailey is based on an original image of Sybil. This appeared on a First Day Postal Cover for Artcraft in 1975.

Incorrect Portrait of Sybil Ludington

This portrait was displayed in the National Women's Museum In the late 1800's, identifying this person as Sybil Ludington. It is an 1801 Watercolor on Ivory of Eliza Izard Pinckney . by Edward Green Malbone.

Chapter 3

Meet Sybil's Family
Fredericksburg, New York
April 22, 1775

It was now April 22, 1775, three days after the Battle of Lexington and Concord. News in Colonial times travelled slowly. It took a number of days for the rest of the colonies to receive the news about Lexington and Concord and to learn the Revolutionary War had begun.

Colonel Henry Ludington ran a mill and farm in Fredericksburg, Dutchess County, New York. At that time, he and his wife Abigail had seven children. Their first three children were girls. The oldest was Sybil, age fourteen; then came Rebecca, age twelve; and then Mary, who was almost ten years old. They also had four sons: Archibald, who was almost eight years old; Henry, Jr. who was age six; Derick, age four; and Tertullus, age two.

There was a lot of work to do with a big family. The fact that the Ludington's oldest son was only eight years old meant a lot of responsibility fell on their daughter Sybil, the oldest child. Henry often complimented Sybil saying, she was better than having an oldest son.

Larry A. Maxwell

Ludington Mill in Kent (Fredericksburg) New York
This mill was built in 1776 and burned down in 1972.
Putnam County Historian's Collection, Brewster, N.Y.

Working alongside her father, Sybil became a very good horseback rider. Whenever a chore or errand involved using a horse, Sybil was the natural choice. She often took messages, to the Militia, for her father.

On that spring day, Colonel Ludington's wife, Abigail was inside the house doing some needlework. Tertullus was playing next to her. She was startled as the door to their home came flying open with a loud, *Thud!*

Sybil pushed the door open and came running inside. She was excited, as she yelled, "Mother! Mother!"

Abigail stopped her needlework. She looked up at Sybil and asked, "Sybil, my child, what ever has you so excited?"

Colonel Ludington entered the house right behind Sybil. Abigail saw him holding a notice in his hand.

Sybil quickly turned and looked at her father. She was so excited she could hardly contain herself, "Oh, Father! You must tell Mother the news!"

225th Anniversary of Sybil's Ride

Risa Scott portrayed Sybil Ludington for the 225th & 230th Anniversary Celebrations of Sybil's ride. She is standing next to Lake Gleneida, Carmel, N.Y., on the route Sybil Ludington rode.
Gleneida Ave., Carmel, New York – Photograph 2002

Abigail looked at her husband, and asked, "Henry, what is Sybil so excited about?"

Sybil's father was excited but was much calmer than

Sybil. He placed his hand on Abigail's shoulder and gave her the news, "Abigail, the Regulars marched on Lexington and Concord!"

Sybil was so excited, she said, "And the Militia sent them running back to Boston!"

Sybil's father looked at her, smiled and said, "Sybil!"

Abigail seriously looked at her husband. She was very concerned about what she just heard. She wanted to know more details. She said, "Henry?"

He was going to explain what happened, but he could see Sybil was very excited and wanted to give the details. He gave in, looked at her, and said, "Go ahead Sybil."

Sybil was very happy her father allowed her to explain what happened. She spoke quickly and with much excitement, "Oh Mother, Paul Revere!"

She asked her mother, "You do know who Paul Revere is?"

Sybil looked at her, waiting for a response.

Abigail shook her head in agreement, while trying to take care of young Tertullus at the same time. She responded, "Yes Sybil, Paul Revere is one of the leaders of the Sons of Liberty in Boston."

Sybil could hardly contain herself. She started walking around the room as she continued speaking, "Yes Mother! That Paul Revere!"

Sybil became more animated as she described what happened, "Paul Revere, and some other men, rode throughout the whole countryside, warning everyone!"

She looked at her mother and with a big smile on her

face said, "Oh! Mother that is so exciting!"

Sybil's father got in a few words, "Yes, Sybil. And because of those riders, Samuel Adams and John Hancock, two of the most prominent leaders of the Sons of Liberty, escaped."

Sybil interrupted. She was very animated, motioning with her arms, as she said, "And the Militia drove the Regulars, all the way back to Boston!"

Abigail looked at her husband and replied with concern, "Henry! Does this mean the war, which you said was coming, has started?"

Colonel Ludington put his hand on Abigail's shoulder. He then held her close to him as he said, "Yes, Abigail, it looks like war has started."

Abigail put a hand to her head in concern.

Henry continued, "The Sons of Liberty have asked all the colonies to send help to Boston."

Abigail looked up and said, "Oh, My!"

Sybil paced about. She looked at her father and said, "Oh, Father! I wish I could have been there and been one of those riders! You know I am a good rider."

She paused, then spoke acting like she was riding, "And I, I would have ridden so hard and told everyone, The Regulars are coming! The Regulars are coming!"

Abigail looked at Sybil. She could barely say anything but one word, "Sybil!"

Colonel Ludington called Sybil over to him and Abigail. He put his other arm around Sybil and said, "Abigail, you know Sybil has always wanted to be a heroine on horseback ever since she heard how our friend Mehitable Prendergast rode eighty miles from up here all the way to New York City, in one day, to save her husband William's life, back during the Settler's Revolt."

Sybil spoke excitedly. "Oh yes, Father. I know I would make a great heroine! I can ride faster and harder and longer than any boy I know!"

Her father agreed and smiled as he looked proudly at Sybil, "Sybil, you are a wonderful daughter. And, I am sure you would make a wonderful heroine. And, it is true, I have not met many boys who can ride as good as you."

Colonel Ludington smiled as he drew Sybil closer to him. He continued speaking. "I am sure you will do a fine job when you are needed."

He grew more serious as he continued speaking, "There are surely going to be dark and dangerous days ahead for us. And, I would not be surprised that one day, you may need to make such a ride, here in New York."

He looked at Sybil and proudly smiled as he said, "And you will be my special heroine!"

Sybil glowed with pride and joyfully replied, "Oh Yes, Father! That would be wonderful!"

A look of intense concern came across Abigail's face as she said, "Oh, Henry!"

 ## Chapter 4

A Plan to End the War
British Headquarters in New York City
March 1, 1777

After Lexington and Concord, a call was sent throughout the colonies asking people to come help drive the British Forces back into the sea. Hundreds responded.

On June 17, 1775, they made a brave stand on Breed's Hill. The battle became known as the Battle of Bunker Hill. Though the Rebels were pushed off the hill by the Crown Forces, they were encouraged by the serious damage they caused the enemy.

The Continental Congress responded and formed an army. They appointed George Washington, from Virginia, as Commander. Soldiers came from many of the different colonies. They helped the Militia surround Boston and kept the Crown Forces trapped.

In March 1776, the Crown Forces sailed away, leaving Boston. Some people were happy thinking the conflict was over. George Washington knew better.

Larry A. Maxwell

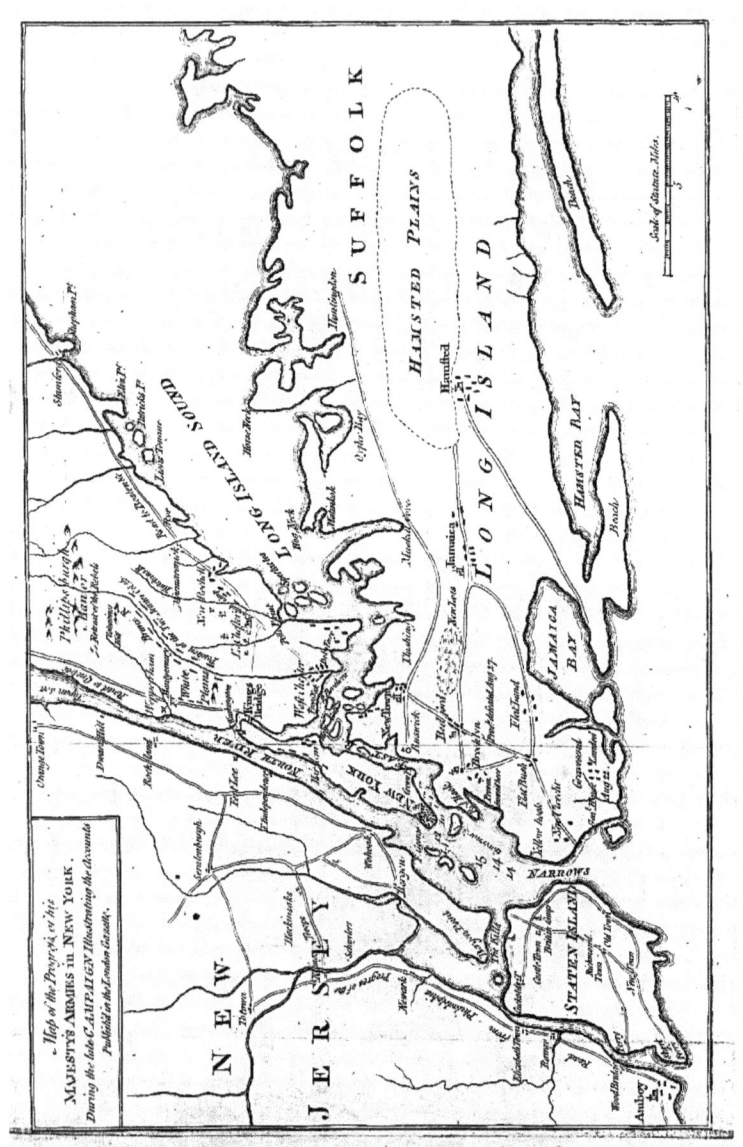

1776 British Map of New York City

*After the British Took Control of New York City.
Lord William Howe's Headquarters were in lower New York City.*
Published in the London Gazette in 1776

In June 1776, the Crown Forces invaded New York. In just a few months they overpowered the poorly equipped Rebels and occupied New York City.

It was now March 1, 1777. British Commander General, The Lord William Howe, came up with a plan to end the war. He called some key officers to his headquarters in New York City. That included General William Erskine, and Governor William Tryon.

Before the war, Tyron served as the Royal Governor of North Carolina, then as Royal Governor of New York. When the Rebellion started, the Rebels replaced him.

When General Erskine and Governor Tryon arrived, Howe was standing at a desk looking at a map with General James Agnew, and General Montfort Browne.

Howe introduced General Agnew, whom they knew. He then said, "May I introduce to you, General Montfort Browne, Royal Governor of the Bahamas and Commander of the new Prince of Wales Loyal American Regiment."

While Governor of the Bahamas, Browne was captured by the Rebels. While a prisoner, he raised the Prince of Wales Loyal American Regiment, to oppose the Rebels.

Browne loved to talk about himself. He also loved to meet anyone he believed might help advance his career. He said, "Gentlemen, it is a pleasure to meet both of you."

After the introductions, Lord Howe called the men to look at a map on his table. He said, "I believe the best way we can end this conflict, is to divide the Rebels right here, along the Hudson River."

Larry A. Maxwell

Portrait of The Lord William Howe
*Portrait by Richard Purcell. Published May 10, 1778.
This bears a very strong resemblance to the portraits published by
Thomas Hart in 1776 of other famous Americans during the
Revolution. All of Hart's portraits are considered fictitious.
It is possible Hart copied Purcell's work.*
On Display at the National Portrait Gallery, London

Portrait of Sir William Erskine

Portrait by Samuel William Reynolds.
Unlike most military uniforms, which had only decorative button holes, Erskine's uniform had working button holes.
On display at the National Portrait Gallery, London.

Portrait of Governor William Tryon

*Some scholars believe this is not William Tryon.
The regimental coat is incorrect.*
On display in Tryon Palace in New Bern, North Carolina.

He look up at them and said, "It is time to divide the troublemakers in New England, and that blasted rabble on the east side of the Hudson River, from the rest of the Rebels on the other side of the Hudson. With their forces divided, they will not be able to last for long."

Erskine saw the logic in Howe's plan. He responded, "Lord Howe, that sounds like a truly excellent idea!"

Howe continued, "General Browne has secured some very important information, information I believe will help us reach our objective and help bring an end to this infernal Rebellion."

When Tryon heard the word, *Rebellion,* he squeezed his fist and said, "I would love to crush this Rebellion, as soon as possible!"

Browne patted Tryon on the shoulder. Tryon was uncomfortable with that physical contact from him.

Browne agreed that he wanted to see the rebellion end as soon as possible. He added, "It is simply too cold here in New York. And I do not know how anyone in their right mind can live here. I would really like to get this whole affair over with, so I can go back to my old post in Bermuda."

Tryon and Erskine were uncomfortable with Browne's attitude. They looked at each other, rolling their eyes.

Howe motioned to a man who had been seated quietly off to the side with a drink in his hand. He said to Browne, "Would you please introduce your guest?

Browne proudly said, "Gentlemen, may I introduce to you the honorable Dr. Jonathan Prosser from Fredericksburg, New York. Dr. Prosser is a very loyal subject of the Crown, and one of my most trusted informants."

Prosser came over to the map. He leaned forward and pointed to the map as he spoke, "I am sure you are aware of the Rebel Supply Depot, over here at Fishkill."

Tryon already knew that information. He said, "Yes, I know, Fishkill very well. It is very close to the Hudson River. And is a very important Rebel Supply Depot."

He then added, "And it is very well defended."

Van Wyck Homestead – Fishkill Supply Depot
*Located on Route 9 in Fishkill, New York.
During the Revolutionary War, the Van Wyck Homestead was the headquarters for the Continental Army's Fishkill Supply Depot.*
Photograph by Larry A. Maxwell - 2017

Browne had a smile on his face the whole time. He thought he knew something Tryon did not know.

Prosser said, "I am not sure if you are aware of this, but the Rebels have another supply depot."

He then pointed to a place on the map and said, "Over here in Danbury, Connecticut."

Tryon nodded in agreement, as he said, "Yes, I am

familiar with that depot in Danbury, it is small and insignificant."

That response made Browne smile. He was glad he knew something Tryon did not know. He proudly said, "That is exactly what they want you to think!"

Browne smiled and encouraged Prosser to continue, "Dr. Prosser, tell them what you discovered."

Prosser continued, "The Rebels know you know Fishkill is their main supply depot, and that you know Danbury is insignificant."

He pointed at the map and continued, "So, assuming you would ignore Danbury, they moved a very large amount of supplies from Fishkill to Danbury."

Browne interrupted and said with a proud smile, "And, they have no idea we know this!"

Tryon and Erskine disliked Browne because of his attitude. But both nodded in approval at what they could see was important information he helped provide.

Howe stepped forward. He said, "Gentlemen, as I said earlier, if we are going to end this Rebellion then we must take control of the Hudson River."

He added firmly, "To take control of the Hudson we must cut off the Rebel's supplies."

Tryon agreed but raised a concern, "I agree that striking the Rebel's supplies is an excellent idea but what about Henry Ludington and the Dutchess County Militia?"

Colonel Henry Ludington, who was Sybil's father, and with his Militia, were not far from Fishkill. They opposed Tryon and his Crown Forces.

Browne upset Tryon by saying, "If I were in charge of the other Loyalist Regiments in this area, we would have apprehended that Ludington and crushed his Militia, a long time ago!"

Tryon explained how he offered a reward of three hundred guineas to anyone who could capture Ludington.

The mention of that reward made Prosser's eyes light up with greed. He asked, "Did you say you are offering a bounty of three hundred guineas for the capture of Colonel Ludington?"

Tryon replied, "Yes, I did, three hundred guineas, dead or alive!

Prosser rubbed his hands together at the idea of getting that reward. He was surprised at the size of the reward, "That is almost a whole year's wages!"

With an evil look in his eye Prosser's said, "For three hundred guineas, I think I can assure you a new guest on one of your prison ships."

Prosser wanted to set out to fulfill his evil deed. He asked to be excused, "If my services are no longer required here, I would like to get to work on my next task, capturing the Rebel, Colonel Henry Ludington!"

Browne escorted Prosser to the door. He spoke to him on the way, "Thank you Dr. Prosser, you have been quite helpful, and I know you are going to be even more helpful."

Browne smiled, then said, "Perhaps you could do two tasks at the same time."

He said to Prosser, "Why not gather your friends, capture that Rebel Ludington, bring him here and join my regiment at the same time?"

He placed his hand on Prosser's shoulder as he said, "I could use more officers like you."

Prosser liked that offer. He replied, "That sounds like a very good idea General Browne."

Browne went back to the table to join the other officers.

Howe continued, "Gentlemen, I have given much thought to what General Browne and Dr. Prosser have shown us."

He pointed to the map and said, "I did not want to be too specific with Dr. Prosser here, but I believe, with all this information before us, the next step to ending this Rebellion is to strike them right here, at Danbury."

Tryon looked to Howe and asked, "That sounds like a very good idea. What do you have in mind?"

Howe turned to Browne, "General Browne, tell them what we discussed."

Browne spoke with pride, "Danbury is about twenty-five miles north of the coastal town of Norwalk."

He pointed to the map as he spoke, "There is only a small contingent of Continentals and Militia on guard at Danbury. If we land here at Compo Beach in Norwalk, we could march to Danbury in one day."

He smiled with a big smile as he said, "We then take, or destroy their supplies, and return to the beach and our ships before the Rebels know what hit them."

Erskine spoke up, "I like that plan. The Rebels would be unaware and unprepared for a strike like that. They would never even consider the fact we would march that far inland for an attack."

Howe continued, "General Browne has many subjects loyal to the Crown between Norwalk and Danbury, so it presents a fairly easy target."

Browne proudly said, "My Loyalists know that country well, and with the help of me and my men, we will be able to get those supplies out of the hands of the Rebel scum and deliver them safely back into the hands of our King!"

Howe pointed to the map and said, "If we can cut off those supplies, here in Danbury, then we will drive a wedge between New England and the rest of the colonies."

He paused, then firmly said, "And resistance will crumble!"

Tryon smiled and responded, "Lord Howe, I do believe that will work!"

Howe then said, "Governor Tryon, I know you deserve vindication, especially since the Rebels stopped recognizing you are their lawful Governor over New York."

Browne agreed with Lord Howe. He did not like the idea that Rebels would dishonor another British official.

Howe continued, "Yes, and so Governor Tryon, I am putting you in charge of the attack on the Rebel Supply Depot at Danbury."

Browne was shocked. He thought he would be leading the attack. He said, "But ... I ..."

Tryon looked at Browne with a smile. He then turned and looked at Lord Howe and responded, "Sir, I would be honored."

Chapter 5

Enoch Crosby the Spy
Fredericksburg, New York
March 2, 1777

It was now March 2, 1777, a cold, chilly winter day in the Hudson Valley. People were gathered in a log church in Fredericksburg, New York. The people sang one last song, then the church service ended.

A few moments later the minister opened the door. Sybil Ludington and her sister Rebecca came outside. She was quickly outside followed by Jesse Ganong. The three of them headed off together toward an old tree.

Jacob Angevine and his son Joseph exited the church. Jacob was a freed slave who earned his freedom, and freedom for his family. It happened when he nearly died saving the life of his former owner, during the French and Indian War. He lost partial use of his left leg. He told everyone he would rather walk with a limp as a free man than be a healthy slave.

Shortly after returning from the war Jacob's joy turned to sorrow. His wife Sarah, and his daughter Elizabeth, became sick with the cholera. Those were dark days. Jacob found hope and strength in his faith and from friends like the Ludington's. Abigail Ludington helped take care of Sarah and Elizabeth until the end.

Jacob joined Colonel Ludington's Militia. Because of his bad leg he was not able to go off to battle. Each time the Militia went to war, Jacob stayed behind helping the Ludington's. He took extra turns patrolling around town.

Colonial Log Church

The Ludingtons attended a church similar to this.
National Register of Historic Places

Jacob taught his son the importance of freedom and the necessity of being willing to fight for it. He was very proud when Joseph joined the Militia.

As they came out of the church, Jacob stopped for a moment and spoke to his son, "Joseph, my son, I am very proud of the way you joined the Militia and are helping to fight for our liberty and freedom."

Jacob stopped speaking for a moment. He looked up toward Heaven, nodded his head, and smiled as he looked back at Jacob. He said, "Your mother would have been very proud of you too."

Joseph was glad he made his father proud. He looked at his father and said, "Thank you father. I will never forget the way you served this country and how you almost died to win our freedom."

Joseph paused, looked up toward Heaven for a moment. Then he looked back at his father and continued, "And I think of Mother and Elizabeth often. I know one day we will all be together again. Until then, I will never take freedom for granted!"

Joseph saw Sybil, Rebecca, and Jesse, near one of the trees. He stared in their direction with a longing look.

Jacob noticed how Sybil and her friends caught his son's attention. He smiled, then faked a cough as he leaned on his walking stick. He weakly spoke, "I imagine you would like to leave your crippled old man and go over to your friends."

Joseph turned around to make sure his father was okay. He saw the smile on his father's face and realized he was teasing.

Jacob waved his walking stick. He pointed toward Sybil and the others as he said, "Get yourself over there."

Sybil was now sixteen years old, Rebecca was fourteen. Joseph and Jesse were both seventeen. The boys were both friends with Sybil and Rebecca. They both had an interest in being more than just friends with Sybil. She also liked the idea of being more than friends. She just did not know which one she liked better. She also liked to tease them. That was a trait she picked up from her father.

Joseph joined Sybil, Rebecca, and Jesse as they talked and played near one of the trees. It was obvious Joseph was excited about being in the Militia. Jesse wanted to join the Militia, but his father would not allow him.

Sybil picked up a stick and spoke as she walked around the tree, "So, what did you think about the preacher's sermon about Queen Esther today?"

A look of anger came across Jesse's face as he answered, "Whenever I hear anyone say the word *King* or *Queen,* it reminds me of King George, and I get so angry I cannot think of anything else except of the injustice that *King* has put us through!"

Joseph stood next to Jesse. He also got an angry look on his face and agreed with Jesse, "I feel the same way!"

Sybil stomped her feet, looked at the boys and said, "Is that all you can think about?!"

Jesse smiled, then spoke as he looked at Sybil, "No, Sybil, sometimes I think about a pretty girl I know, who loves to ride horses."

Sybil and Rebecca smiled and giggled.

Joseph wanted Sybil to know he was interested in her too. He quickly said, "Me too!"

Jesse continued, "Yes, I do wish I could see that girl come back around these parts sometime."

Rebecca giggled, Sybil stuck out her tongue at Jesse.

Sybil then said, "Well, I did listen to the preacher today and I love the story of Esther. She was a real heroine! She was a woman who made a difficult decision and helped save her people just like I will do one day!"

Joseph agreed, "Oh, and I am sure you would be a lovely heroine!"

He smiled, bowed to Sybil and said, "Queen Sybil!"

Jesse laughed and joined in the fun, "Ah, but you know what we do to royalty around here?"

Joseph grabbed a long stick from the ground. He found another long one and threw it to Jesse. Jesse pointed the stick at Sybil and said, "We shoot them!"

Joseph and Jesse pretended the sticks were muskets and shot at Sybil and Rebecca. Rebecca smiled and ducked. Sybil ducked, then shook her head and laughed.

Sybil then acted like she was riding her horse, as she said, "There will be no shooting royalty until the heroine rides and calls out the Militia!"

Jesse and Joseph laughed and lined up like Militia. They held the sticks at their shoulders, as though they were muskets. Rebecca lined up next to them.

Jesse got a big smile on his face, "Yes, Miss Revere!"

As Sybil, Rebecca, Joseph, and Jesse continued to laugh and play, Henry and Abigail Ludington, Sybil's parents, came out of church. They were followed by John and Mary Ganong, Jesse's parents.

The Ganongs were business people who had dealings with others who liked the Crown. They did not consider themselves Loyalists yet wished the Revolution would end. They wanted things to go back to the way they were before the conflict started.

John Ganong tipped his hat, and greeted Henry and his wife Abigail, "Greetings, Colonel Ludington, Mrs. Ludington."

Abigail gave a small curtsey. Henry took his hat off, "Greetings John."

He bowed to Mrs. Ganong and said, "Mary."

John was troubled. With a look of concern on his face, he said, "Colonel Ludington, I heard Governor Tyron placed a bounty on your head!"

Henry replied, "Yes, John I did hear that. I wonder what took him so long?"

John was not amused at Henry's comments. He sternly replied, "Henry!"

Henry acted like he was sorry but was not. He said, "Sorry John. And did you say Governor Tryon? May I remind you, he is now the *former Governor*."

John was upset with Henry's comments, "But Henry! Governor Tryon is a general in the British Army, and he has the whole weight of the Crown behind him!"

Henry jokingly said, "That is true. So, John, were you thinking of collecting the bounty? I am sure three hundred guineas would be a nice prize for you to collect!"

John said, "Henry! You know I would not do that!"

Henry gave John a friendly slap on the back. Then he said, "Yes, I know, John, after all you and I did fight side-by-side in the French and Indian War."

John said, "Yes, we did! But we fought as loyal subjects of the Crown! Against the French and the Indians!"

Henry teasingly said, "John, are you trying to persuade me to switch sides? Do you want me to become a Tory?"

John did not consider himself a Loyalist but was concerned with the actions of Henry's friends in the Continental Congress. He said, "Henry, please be serious. You know I signed the Oath of Allegiance, just like you. But I am concerned! I am concerned where this is going! It was one thing to want representation, but now! Now, we have the whole British army here!"

John was concerned for his future. "Remember what they did to New York City?"

The Crown Forces arrested those they considered Rebels,. They took away their homes and burned their churches. He was fearful that may happen to them.

John continued, "And now, the Continental Congress has sent Benjamin Franklin to France, seeking to form an alliance with the very people you and I fought against! "

Henry smiled and said, "That is true. Franklin is in France negotiating with our old enemy. Could you imagine if he could get the French to join us? The French on our side? Now that could make a big difference."

Henry's words upset John, "For God's sake Henry! It seems like everything is getting out of hand! I have always held out hope that somehow we could peacefully reconcile our differences with the Crown, but now!"

John continued, "Now, they have placed a reward of three hundred guineas on your head! And, they say the reward is dead or alive! I fear for you and your family! And for mine! And for where all this is headed!"

As they were speaking, Enoch Crosby rode up. He rode slowly past Sybil, Rebecca, Jesse, and Joseph. He tipped his hat as he passed by the children.

Portrait of Enoch Crosby When Older
By Samuel Lovett Waldo & William Jewett, 1830.
Smithsonian National Portrait Gallery

Joseph looked at Crosby with a sneer. He then spoke to the others with disgust, "Oh! I cannot stand that man!"

Jesse asked, "Who is that?"

Sybil answered, "That is Enoch Crosby."

Joseph wanted to make sure Jesse knew Crosby was a bad person. He said, "He is one of those awful people with Tory sympathies!"

An angry look came across Jesse's face as he said, "You mean like my father?"

Joseph was concerned he offended Jesse. He said, "Sorry Jesse, I did not mean to offend you."

Jesse said, "Joseph, you did not offend me. It is those Tories, and people who try to sit on the fence, like my father, who offend me!"

He was clearly angry as he said, "And, if that Enoch Crosby is one of them, then this is what I think of him." Jesse then spit on the ground.

Sybil was concerned. She knew Crosby was not a Loyalist. She knew he was a spy for the Continentals but could not say that. She changed the subject and said, "He sure does have a nice horse!"

Joseph looked at her angrily and said, "Sybil! Is that all you think about? Horses?"

Sybil smiled as she spoke, teasing him, "What else is there to think about? Boys?"

She then pushed her way past Joseph and Jesse. She and Rebecca laughed as they walked away. The boys smiled and shook their heads.

Enoch Crosby got off his horsed and walked toward Colonel Henry and Abigail Ludington. They were still talking with John and Mary Ganong.

As Crosby came closer, Henry welcomed him, "Greetings Enoch!"

John Ganong warmly welcomed him, "Greetings, Mr. Crosby! It is so nice to see someone with some good sense here."

Crosby responded with a nod and a bow, "And greetings to you, John, Colonel Ludington and your lovely wives."

The Ladies smiled and did a small curtsey in response.

Crosby looked at the others and said, "Would you please excuse me, I need to speak with Henry for a moment."

John was hoping Crosby would try to convince Henry to rethink things and see things his way. He said, "Enoch, see if you can talk some sense into him."

Knowing John's positions, Crosby smiled,. He acted like they were on the same side and said, "I shall, John."

As Henry and Enoch stepped aside, Henry said, "Enoch, it must be hard having everyone think you have Loyalist sympathies."

Crosby nodded yes, but explained his position, "Yes, Henry. Sometimes it is hard being misunderstood, but we need eyes and ears in the enemy camp and that role has fallen upon me. Let them think of me what they will, I am willing to be misunderstood for the sake of liberty."

Henry looked around making sure no one else was listening. Then he said, "So, I assume you have some news for me?"

Enoch showed concern on his face as he said, "Yes, Henry, and it is not good news."

Crosby leaned closer and said, "Governor Tryon has put a bounty of three hundred guineas on your head."

Henry already knew that news. He said, "John and I were just discussing that."

Crosby was surprised. He asked, "You already heard?"

Henry nodded his head. Then he said, "Yes, Enoch, that kind of news travels fast!"

Crosby showed extreme concern as he said, "Henry, a bounty of three hundred guineas! Dead or alive! That is almost a whole year's wages!"

Henry smiled and jokingly said, "I am honored!"

Having compared the reward to the amount of money Judas received for betraying Jesus, "I thought the bounty would have been for thirty pieces of silver!"

Crosby urged concern, "Henry, you are going to have to be very careful. I know some Judases in these parts who would gladly have betrayed you for thirty pieces of silver, but now for three hundred guineas! I think now they will surely seek to collect that reward."

Henry showed he understood, "Yes, Enoch, that is true. I will be on my guard."

Henry smiled and jokingly said, "Three hundred guineas!"

Enoch punched Henry knowing he was kidding.

Chapter 6

The Loyalists Plot
March 4, 1777

After learning of the large bounty for capturing Henry Ludington, Dr. Jonathan Prosser wanted to find a way to collect that reward. He wanted to become an officer in General Montfort Browne's Loyalist Regiment. He went back to Dutchess County as fast as he could. He knew he needed help to carry out his plan. He also knew it would be difficult because there were few Loyalists there.

Loyalists were rounded up and arrested by Colonel Ludington, who was a member of the Committee of Safety in Dutchess County. Some were convinced to sign an Oath of Loyalty to the Rebel cause.

Dr. Prosser knew some signed the Oath because they were too far away to receive help from the Crown. They did not want to be arrested for not signing the oath. He wanted to locate those people.

He believed he could convince some people to side with him if he gave them a share in the reward or the chance of getting their neighbor's land.

Drumming Out of Town
Loyalist were arrested or drummed out of many towns.
18th Century Engraving

Prosser knew he had to act quickly. He also knew he could be arrested so he was very careful. He finally arranged a meeting at a tavern with David Chase and Roger Cutler. They were two men he knew were Loyalists

The three met and sat in the far corner of the tavern. They tried to make sure no one else could overhear them. When Prosser felt it was safe, he spoke.

"I am sick of these Rebels!" he said. "This revolution of theirs has made life extremely difficult for us loyal subjects of the Crown!"

Chase and Cutler agreed, "Here, here!"

Prosser showed his disgust for the Rebels as he said, "I have seen those disloyal scoundrels throw too many people in jail and piously say it is in the name of liberty!"

He spit on the ground and said, "Liberty! All they want is the liberty to ignore our gracious King and liberty to take away our land and our homes!"

Cutler said, "If I had my way, they would all be hung!"

Chase asked, "Dr. Prosser, I do not see why the King does not send his forces up here and crush them once and for all."

Prosser nodded his head in agreement. He leaned close and said, "I have some news I know you will like."

He got an evil smile on his face and said, "David, Roger, the Crown Forces have a plan to come up here and crush the Rebels!"

Chase was surprised. He asked, "Really?"

"Yes, David," Prosser said, affirming what he said.

Prosser looked around again to make sure no one else was listening. Then he quietly said, "They plan to attack the Rebel depots and destroy their supplies."

With a look of surprise, Cutler asked, "Dr. Prosser, are you sure?"

Prosser smiled pridefully. He said, "Yes, Roger, I am quite sure. I personally brought the information about the Rebel Supply Depot at Danbury to General Browne, of the Loyal American Regiment. And he brought me before the Lord William Howe!"

Cutler and Chase looked at each other with their mouths open in awe.

Prosser spoke proudly, "The Lord Howe then summoned Governor Tryon, General Agnew and General Erskine and had me tell all of them about Danbury. They discussed both the Fishkill and the Danbury supply depots and said they must launch an attack."

Cutler was so excited to hear that. He said, "That is great news!"

Prosser continued, "Roger, it gets even better. That attack will take place, within the month!"

Cutler and Chase were very pleased. They eagerly took another drink from their mugs.

Inside a Colonial Tavern
Published by Carrington Bowles, 1766-1799.

"The day has finally come," Prosser said. "General Browne wants us to gather as many men as we can and wants us to come to New York to join his Loyalist Regiment, so we can help them defeat the Rebels and reclaim our country!"

This was better than either Cutler or Chase expected.

Prosser asked, "Are you with me?"

Cutler and Chase looked at each other, then at

Prosser. Then they loudly said, "Yes!"

Prosser looked around and motioned for them to be quiet. He leaned closer and spoke quietly, "Now, there is one last very special thing I need to tell you. Lord Howe and General Browne, would like us to do one more thing, before we go join General Browne's Regiment."

Cutler asked, "What is that?"

Prosser replied, "Governor Tryon has placed a bounty of three hundred guineas on the head of that blasted Rebel Colonel Henry Ludington."

The large size of the bounty excited Chase and Cutler. They could not imagine a reward that large. Chase said, "Three hundred guineas?!"

Cutler added, "That is a whole year's worth of wages!"

Chase smiled and said, "I would love some of that money."

"Yes, David, I would too," Cutler said. He looked at his mug, then said, "That would buy me a lot of rum!"

They laughed at the thought of having all that money.

Chase got a serious look on his face. He leaned closer and asked, "So, Dr. Prosser, what were you thinking?"

Prosser looked very seriously at them. Then he said, "Roger, David, I have a plan."

He got an evil smile on his face as he explained his plan. "We can capture Colonel Ludington and bring him to New York as our prize when we go to enlist!"

Chase and Cutler loved that idea. Chase said, "I like that idea, but how do we do that?"

Prosser revealed his plan, "I have muskets hidden

safe in the Great Swamp. I want you both to gather as many men as you can, those loyal to the Crown."

He paused, leaned in close and said, "We will meet in the swamp, get the muskets and then go to Ludington's house at night, overwhelm the guards, capture him and take him with us to New York City as our prize!"

Cutler and Chase were very pleased to see Prosser had a very specific, well thought out plan.

Cutler smiled as he picked up his mug, He said, "I can almost taste the rum of victory!"

They all laughed and took another drink.

Prosser knew they must act fast. He urged them to take immediate action. "Now, get to it! Find others to help us! We have no time to waste!"

Cutler and Chase were so excited they almost tripped over each other as they got up to leave. Prosser stayed at the table to finish his drink.

As Cutler and Chase were leaving, Enoch Crosby arrived. They believed Crosby had Loyalist sympathies. They politely nodded to him and they left.

Prosser noticed Crosby enter. He called him to come over to his table, "Enoch! Come over here!"

Crosby walked over to Prosser. As he approached, he tipped his hat, "Greetings, Dr. Prosser."

Prosser replied to Crosby with a friendly nod of his head, "Enoch, it is so good to see you. Please, have a seat."

Crosby sat down at the table. He said, "Thank you, Dr. Prosser, the pleasure is all mine."

Prosser was glad to see Crosby because he believed

Crosby had strong Loyalist leanings, just like him. He did not know Crosby was a spy for the Continentals.

An evil smile came across Prosser's face. He said to Crosby, "I have some great news for you, my friend."

Crosby responded, "Yes?"

Prosser smiled. He took another drink, then said, "Enoch, this Rebellion will be over soon."

Crosby smiled, acting as though he liked what Prosser was saying. He asked, "That is good news, but what makes you say that?"

Prosser looked around the room, to make sure no one was listening. He then leaned in closer to Crosby and softly said, "The British army is going to launch a raid to destroy the Rebel's Supply Depot."

That news troubled Crosby, He looked at Prosser and asked, "Are you sure?"

Prosser nodded. He leaned closer and said, "Yes! I heard it directly from The Lord Howe and General Browne!"

Crosby looked surprised at what he heard Prosser say. He asked, "Directly?"

Prosser was proud of the meeting he had and the news he bore. He proudly said, "Yes! I had the honor of meeting with them personally and I brought them information about the Rebel Supply Depots."

Though Crosby was quite upset at that news, he acted very pleased. He looked at Prosser and said, "Oh, you did? I imagine, they must have been pleased with that."

Prosser said, "Yes! They were very pleased, and they

told me they plan to attack within the month!"

Crosby was listening intently. He wanted more details. He asked, "Any idea where they plan to attack?"

Prosser was unsure but answered. "I am not sure about that. It could be Danbury or Fishkill. They are both Rebel Supply Depots."

Crosby was concerned. He was hoping for more information. He replied, "Yes, they are."

Prosser said, "Though I gave them more information about Danbury, I would not be surprised if they strike at Fishkill."

Crosby wanted to know which depot the Crown Forces intended to attack. He asked, "What makes you think they will attack Fishkill?"

Prosser said, "Governor Tryon was there, at that meeting with me. He said he knows Fishkill is the bigger depot. He said this attack would deal a major blow to the Rebels seeing their depot attacked."

Prosser attempted some humor using a play on words, "Why not kill the fish at Fishkill?!"

Crosby forced a laugh, "Oh, yes."

Prosser leaned closer to Crosby. He said. "Enoch, a number of us are going to go join General Browne's Loyalist Regiment, so we can help with the attack and finally put an end to this infernal Rebellion."

Prosser put his hand on Crosby's arm. He smiled and said, "Enoch, you are such a fine Loyalist. I would be honored to have you come with us."

Crosby was upset but acted honored at the invitation.

He was pleased Prosser had no idea about his true loyalties. He replied, "Dr. Prosser, that is very tempting."

Crosby came up with a good response to not participate. He said, "But, someone needs to stay behind and keep an eye on things."

He then winked and smiled as he looked at Prosser. He said, "If you know what I mean?"

Prosser smiled at Crosby's reply. He said, "Excellent idea, Enoch, excellent idea!"

They both laughed. Prosser leaned in close and spoke softer, "Now there is one thing more."

Crosby listened more intently, "I pray, do tell me."

Prosser told him of his plan to capture Colonel Henry Ludington. "We are going to apprehend that wretched Rebel Henry Ludington and collect the three hundred guineas reward on his head!"

Crosby acted like he was taken back but he expected something like this. He acted pleased with Prosser's idea. He said, "Oh, my! That is quite a lot of money."

Prosser smiled and said "Indeed it is. Capturing that blasted Ludington will dishearten his band of Rebels and it will be a due reward for those of us who have been faithful to the Crown, we who have suffered such indignity at his hands!"

Crosby acted pleased with Prosser's plan and said, "You really are quite a Loyalist!"

Prosser was proud. He laughed and said, "Yes, I am!"

They laughed again. Prosser missed the glimpse of concern on Crosby's face.

Chapter 7

Crosby Warns Ludington
March 5, 1777

It was now March 5, 1777, a cold winter day outside the Ludington's home. Colonel Henry Ludington was working hard splitting wood. Wood was the only source of heat in their home back then.

Jacob and Joseph Angevine, the Ludington's good friends, stopped by to help. Joseph was young and strong and good with an axe. He started splitting wood with the Colonel. Jacob was not able to do it because of his disabled leg. Instead, he picked up and stacked the wood.

The Colonel did not want to be outdone by Joseph. Each time Joseph split a log he also split one. Soon, it looked like they were having a log splitting contest, trying to see who could split the most logs.

Sybil, Rebecca, and Mary picked up the pieces of wood, which Joseph split. Jacob, Archibald, and Henry Jr. picked up the wood the Colonel split. Some went back and forth, taking wood inside the house.

The Colonel stopped and wiped the sweat off his brow. He said, "Joseph, you are very handy with that axe!

Larry A. Maxwell

An Integrated Militia

The Militia and Army on both sides were integrated during the Revolution. After the Revolution, the stupidity of segregation became a part of the military until the Korean War.
Living History Guild Photograph

Joseph stopped. He was tired and glad the Colonel took that break. He pointed his axe at his father and replied, "I had a good teacher."

Jacob paused, holding an arm full of split wood. With a big smile on his face he said, "And if my leg had not been shattered at Fort William Henry, I would have split twice as much wood as both of you!"

The Colonel smiled as he looked at Jacob and Joseph and said, "Jacob, I really appreciate you and Joseph coming by to help us split this wood. We used up most of our wood this winter and the war has kept me away from home more than I would like."

Jacob replied, "I wish I could do more to help with the

fight. I am so glad I earned my freedom from slavery. Now I look at this war as a struggle to help others become free from tyranny."

Henry said, "This war is indeed a struggle and you do more than your fair share Jacob. And It means a lot to me to know I have someone brave and reliable like you, to help keep things safe around here while I am gone."

Sybil was picking up wood. Her father's remarks made her speak up, "And what about me? Are you glad you have me around to help, when you are gone?"

Rebecca was picking up a piece of wood. She stood up next to Sybil and quickly asked, "And me too?!"

Soon all the children said, "What about me?!"

The Colonel looked at each one and said, "Yes! I am very glad for you, and you, and you, and you and for you."

That made them all smile.

As they were talking, Enoch Crosby came riding up the road. He had a serious look on his face.

Sybil saw him coming before her father did. She called out, "Oh Father, Look! It is Mr. Enoch Crosby!"

Enoch Crosby was a good friend of her father. Everyone liked it when he came for a visit.

Crosby had a very important message for Colonel Ludington. He rode up close to where the Colonel was. He got off his horse and tied it to the fence.

Colonel Ludington put down his axe. He greeted Crosby with a warm handshake. "Enoch!"

Crosby smiled and returned the greeting, "Henry!"

Jacob and Joseph were surprised to see Enoch

Crosby. They believed he was a Loyalist. They did not like him and the side they thought he choose. They walked off to the side with a look of disapproval on their faces.

Crosby did not take notice of them. He tried to greet all the Ludington children by name. It was something he did each time he came. Each one smiled and did a curtsey or bow when he got their name right.

He looked at the two oldest girls and said "Hello Sybil! Hello Rebecca!"

He looked at the third daughter. He waited a moment. Then he said, "Mary!"

The girls smiled when he got all their names right.

Crosby looked at Archibald and said, "Umm, Henry?"

That was not his name. Archibald shook his head, *No!*

Henry, Jr., spoke up, "No! I am Henry!"

Archibald then said, "And I am Archibald!"

Sybil smiled and said, "Mr. Crosby, you always mix up Archibald and Henry!"

The Colonel said, "Sybil, do you remember Mr. Crosby used to mix up you and Rebecca?"

Crosby smiled and said, "Well, sometimes, it is hard to tell such lovely girls apart."

That comment pleased Sybil and Rebecca. They smiled and gave him a curtsey.

The Colonel placed a hand on Sybil's shoulder. Then he looked at Sybil and said, "I never have that problem, do I, Rebecca?"

Sybil shook off her father's hand off. She looked at him sternly, even though she knew he was kidding.

She then smiled and said, "Father!"

Sybil looked at Enoch. She realized he must have come with an important message for their father. It was probably something not for them to hear. She also knew Jacob and Joseph thought Enoch was a Tory and were upset he was there. She came up with an idea. She said, "I think Mr. Crosby has some business to discuss with Father."

Crosby appreciated Sybil's comment. He continued Henry's jest as he looked at Sybil and said, "Yes, Rebecca, I would like to speak with your father alone, if possible."

They all laughed knowing he was jesting when he called Sybil, Rebecca. Everyone laughed except for Jacob and Joseph. Nothing a Tory said could make them smile.

The Colonel spoke to Jacob and Joseph, "Jacob and Joseph, would you please excuse me? I have to complete an important transaction with Mr. Crosby."

Joseph held his axe firmly hoping to scare Enoch. He said to the Colonel, "Would you like me to stay close in case there is any trouble?"

The Colonel picked up his own axe and held it firmly. He nodded to Joseph and said, "I am sure, I will be okay, but if I need you, I will call."

Sybil then called to the others, "Come along, everyone, let us get a drink of water."

That did not seem to work. She added, "And who wants to help me make some cartridges for the muskets?"

The children all responded, "I do! I do!"

Joseph replied, "Yes, I would love to help make some

cartridges, so I can use them on some Tories!"

Jacob was upset Enoch was there but knew Henry would do the right thing. "There will be a time and place for that, Joseph, "he said. "Yet this is not the time, nor the place."

Jacob and Enoch headed to the house.

Enoch tried to hide a smile. He said to Henry, "I am glad to see that young man has no love for Tories."

Henry replied, "That is right, he has no love for Tories. He is very dedicated to the cause and is becoming a fine addition to my Militia. Just make sure you do not encounter him when he has a musket in his hands. After all, you are a notorious Tory!

Enoch smiled and replied, "I will be careful!"

He then changed the subject, "And by the way, you have a delightful family,

Henry smiled, "Yes I do, I am so blessed."

Crosby complimented Sybil, "Sybil sure is growing up to be a fine young woman."

Henry nodded in agreement then added an important fact, "She will be sixteen in just a few short weeks. She is as good to me as having an eldest son."

Crosby said, "I know she has been a good messenger when you need to send messages to the Militia."

Henry said, "Yes, she knows the roads and lanes very well." He then looked at Crosby and said, "But, I am sure you are not here to talk about my wonderful family."

Crosby's said, "That is correct. I just met with Dr. Jonathan Prosser. You know who I mean?"

Henry shook his head yes. He said, "Yes, the Committee of Safety has been keeping an eye on him."

Henry smiled and said in jest, "Of course, the Committee also told me to keep an eye on you."

Crosby smiled. Then he became very serious again, "As long as the right people know where my loyalties lie, and the wrong people do not, that is fine with me."

Henry patted Crosby on the shoulder and nodded his head in agreement.

Crosby got to the reason for his visit, "Dr. Prosser is one of those who thinks my loyalties are with the Crown."

Henry nodded in agreement.

Crosby then told him, "So he told me the British plan to attack our supply depot within the month!"

A look of concern came over Henry's face. He said, "We were expecting something like that."

He paused, then asked, "Did he say whether the raid will be against Fishkill or Danbury?"

Crosby shook his head, and said, "No, he did not say. I do not think he knows which one, and I am not sure if they trust him enough to give him specific information like that."

He then said something he observed, which most Loyalists did not realize, "You know the British Regulars do not really trust their Tory sympathizers. I am sure they are thinking, if the Tories will turn against their own neighbors, maybe one day they will turn against them."

Henry shook his head in agreement.

Crosby continued, "Prosser said the Crown Forces

will be here within the next month. He said he thinks the attack will be on Fishkill because that is the larger depot and it will be more demoralizing if they strike there."

Henry said. "Yes, that would be demoralizing."

With a look of urgency on his face he said, "We must get word to both Danbury and Fishkill, just to be safe!"

Crosby assured Henry he did that, "I already passed the word along to them."

Henry was pleased and relieved to hear that.

Crosby came closer to Henry to give him one more piece of troubling news, "There is one more thing."

Crosby hesitated. Henry saw the look of concern on Crosby's face and asked, "Yes?"

Crosby continued, "Prosser said, he is gathering a group of men to go with him to join General Browne's Loyalist Regiment."

Henry smiled at that news. Then he responded with some sarcasm, "That is good news. That will be a few less people I will have to watch out for."

Crosby smiled and shook his head again. Then continued with a very serious tone, "But, here is the troubling news."

Crosby hesitated again.

Henry asked, "Yes?"

Crosby continued. "Before they go, they plan to get a prize to take with them."

Henry acted like he did not know what Crosby was trying to say.

Crosby said, "They plan to capture one Colonel Henry

Ludington and take him as their prize to British headquarters, where they will collect the three hundred guineas bounty, which is on your head."

Henry smiled,. He took off his hat and acted like he was feeling for the money on his head. He then said, "I do not feel three hundred guineas on my head."

Crosby smiled at Henry's humor. He said, "If I did not know you better Henry, I would think you are not taking this seriously. But I do know you!"

Henry put his hat back on and smiled. He continued with his sarcasm as he stared at Crosby and said, "And I know you too Enoch, and I am keeping my eyes on you, like the Committee of Safety said I should do."

Crosby smiled. He knew Henry realized the message he delivered was very seriousness.

Crosby got back on his horse. Then he said one last thing, "Please take care Henry!"

Henry nodded. He gave Crosby's horse a slap and sent him off, as he said, "God speed, my friend!"

As Crosby rode off, Henry picked up his axe and headed back to the house.

Chapter 8

Attempt to Capture Ludington
March 7, 1777 - Evening

It was March 7, 1777. It was another cold winter night in the Hudson Valley. Loyalist Dr. Jonathan Prosser, David Chase and Roger Cutler rounded up a mob of men to help with their plot. They promised them a profit for their loyalty to the Crown.

Prosser told them about the Crown Forces plan to attack one of the Rebel Supply Depots and bring a quick end to the war. He convinced the men to help him capture Colonel Henry Ludington. They would take him to British headquarters and receive a huge reward. He said they would then join General Montfort Browne's Loyalist Regiment and bring a swift end to the war.

Chase and his men met Prosser in the Great Swamp, where Prosser hid muskets. With torches in hand they began to make their way down the road to apprehend Colonel Ludington. They were happy when they received word the Colonel was home without any Militia around.

As they marched towards the Ludington's, Prosser knew they recruited some who were not the best sort of people. He was concerned one of them would shoot the colonel. He firmly told them, "Remember not to shoot anyone unless it is absolutely necessary."

Loyalists Seek to Apprehend Colonel Ludington
Image by Lyman Abbott, 1850
The Pictorial Field Book to the Revolution

One of the men replied, "Aww! Dr. Prosser, I would really like to shoot that Rebel and get it over with!"

"Yes, let us shoot some Rebels!" one replied.

Some of the men agreed.

Prosser spoke again, "Lord Howe, Commander of His Majesty's Forces prefers we capture Ludington alive. And there is a nice large bounty we will all collect when we bring him in alive. You would like to collect that bounty, would you not?!"

They replied, with a hearty, "Huzzah!"

One of them said, "If I cannot shoot Colonel Ludington, I hope there are some other Rebels I can shoot!"

Prosser replied, "You will have plenty of opportunities to shoot as many Rebels as you want, after we bring Colonel Ludington to Lord Howe."

Prosser then added, "When we turn in Colonel Ludington, we will be rewarded, and become part of General Montfort Browne's Loyalist Regiment. Then you can shoot as many Rebels as you want!"

One of the men wearing an old frock coat asked, "Are they going to give us some nice red coats to wear?"

Prosser was surprised that man was there because he thought he might get a nice uniform. He smiled and replied, "Unlike the Rebel Militia, who have to provide their own clothing and weapons, the Crown will give us nice green uniforms, with white facings. And they will also give us muskets!"

That response made a big smile appear on the face of the man who asked the question.

Prosser then said, "And, when we defeat the Rebels, they will give us all the Rebel's land and houses!"

Some of them had their land seized by the Rebels. They liked the idea of taking away their Rebel neighbor's property. They shouted, "Huzzah!"

After a little while they saw some men approaching with torches. They stopped and waited to see who it was. They were hoping it was not the dreaded Rebel's Committee of Safety, which rounded up Loyalists.

Prosser was relieved when he saw the man leading the group was Roger Cutler. Cutler was thankful he found Prosser and the rest of the men.

Cutler greeted Prosser, "Dr. Prosser, I gathered a few more men, loyal to the Crown."

A big smile came across Prosser's face. He greeted Cutler and said, "Good work, Roger."

Prosser looked at the group of men. He was glad to see Cutler rounded up more men than he expected.

Prosser then spoke to all the men, "Now is the time for us to go get our prize! We will capture that annoying, obnoxious, Rebel, Henry Ludington and take him with us as our prisoner to New York. There he will see what it is like to be in prison for one's beliefs. Then we will receive our reward, join the Loyalist Regiment and help put an end to this cursed Rebellion once and for all!"

He then asked, "Are you with me?!"

Some hesitated but others shouted, "Yes!"

He was glad to see their enthusiasm. He realized they were passing a house where there might be people who might not like what they were saying. That made him nervous. He quickly told the men, "Not so loud!"

When the men saw Prosser looked concerned they looked at each other. They understood it probably was a good idea to be quieter. That made them nervous.

When Prosser saw their nervous looks. He made himself smile then spoke softly, "Long live the King!"

They responded with a quieter, "Long live the King!"

They continued on the road towards the Ludington's.

After walking for a while one man with a deep voice, and strong English accent said, "The Rebels are such an ungrateful lot! They should be grateful the King allows them to pay taxes!"

"That's right!" said another man. "It is an honor to be a subject of the King! And after all, Parliament has every right to tax anyone they want! How else do they expect the Crown to pay for the soldiers to protect us!"

Another said, "And if it were not for those Crown Forces we would have been overrun by the French and all been forced to become Catholics!"

He was referring to the French and Indian War. The French, who were the enemy back then, were mainly Catholic. The British King and Parliament were Anglicans. To scare people, they said the Colonials would be forced to become Catholic if the French won that war.

They keep walking down the road. It seemed like they were walking for hours. Then Prosser had them stop. He signaled for all of them to come close to him.

When they were all close enough to hear him, he said, "We are getting close to Colonel Ludington's, so every one of you put out those torches." He paused, then said, "We do not want them to see us coming."

He then laughed a sinister laugh and said, "We will take them by surprise!"

"Yes, Sir!" many of them replied loudly.

Prosser replied in a firm but quieter voice, "And be quiet! We do not want them to hear we are coming!"

When the torches were put out it became very dark.

Colonial Two-Story Home
Similar to the Ludington's home. Their home had a porch, stone chimneys on each end, an attic, and a side room.
Photograph by Larry A. Maxwell, 2018

Sybil was keeping watch outside of her home. She hid behind a tree with a loaded musket held in her hands, looking, and listening for signs of Tories approaching.

Her father trained her and Rebecca to load and shoot a musket accurately. They were good shots. Any Tory who crossed their paths would be in big trouble.

Sybil heard a sound. She looked down the road and saw something moving. She watched carefully. Finally, she could see the shape of men approaching. She knew men approaching at night, without lit torches, meant trouble. She was concerned but knew exactly what to do. She quickly slipped out from behind the tree. She quietly ran around to the back of the house where her sister Rebecca was keeping guard. Rebecca could tell something was wrong as soon as she saw Sybil.

Sybil quietly, yet firmly said, "Rebecca, quickly, inside, there is a whole group of men coming!"

Prosser and his mob tried to quietly proceed down the

road as they drew closer to the Ludington's home. They did not know they had been detected.

Sybil's mother, Abigail, was seated near the fireplace. She held her baby daughter. Sybil's father was sitting in his chair reading.

As Sybil and Rebecca quickly entered the room, Henry stopped reading. He and Abigail looked up with concern on their faces.

Sybil spoke quietly but with concern, "Father, there is a group of men coming down the road toward the house."

Henry got up. He grabbed his cartridge box and put it on over his shoulder. He then got his pistol and told Sybil and Rebecca, "Wake up your brothers and sisters. It is time for everyone to do as we practiced."

Henry carefully loaded his pistol as Sybil and Rebecca went upstairs. He adjusted the sword on his side.

When Sybil and Rebecca reached the top of the stairs they saw the other children in bed. Sybil and Rebecca quickly and quietly woke up Mary, and their brothers, Archibald and Henry, Jr. As they woke them, Rebecca let them know they needed to be quiet.

Sybil put a finger over her lips. She spoke to them, "Time to get up! Shhh!"

She then said, "Some bad people are coming, and Father needs our help to do what we practiced."

Mary, Archibald and Henry, Jr., rose quickly and quietly out of bed. The younger brothers, Derick and Tertullus they stayed sound asleep.

Sybil said, "Mary, help Rebecca light the candles.

Archibald and Henry, help me get the muskets and hats."

Prosser and his mob of Loyalists were getting close to the house. He had them pause. He was excited their task was going so smoothly. He smiled as he pictured easily capturing the Colonel and getting the big reward.

He smiled as he gave orders, "Roger, take one group and go behind the house, that way. David, you take another group and go behind the house that way. We are not going to let our prize escape! We will surround the house and call for Colonel Ludington to surrender."

At the same time, Rebecca and Mary set candles on top of the furniture, which was against the wall opposite from the windows. Then they lit the candles. The light from the candles created big shadows when they moved between the candles and the windows.

Sybil, Archibald and Henry, Jr., all came back in the room holding a musket and wearing a man's hat. Sybil carried an extra musket and hat. She gave them to Rebecca. Rebecca put the hat on her head and put the musket against her left shoulder, just like the Militia did.

Sybil gave the command, "Now everyone, march back and forth, between the candles and the windows, while Mary makes sure the candles do not go out."

Sybil, Rebecca, Archibald and Henry, Jr., all put muskets on their left shoulders and marched back and forth in front of the windows. With the curtains were closed, their actions cast large shadows on the windows. The shadows were much larger than them. It made it look like there were quite a few men on guard in the house.

Roger Cutler was about to lead his men to the back of the house. He looked up and saw movement in the windows. He froze in fear at what appeared to be soldiers marching upstairs in the house.

Cutler pointed at the windows and spoke with alarm, "Dr. Prosser! Look at the windows!"

Old Postcard of Colonial Bedroom

Most bedrooms were open, with few furnishings. Lit candles on a dresser would cast large shadows on windows.

Dr. Prosser and the others heard the fear in Cutler's voice. He quickly looked up at the house. They were horrified when they saw what appeared to be many soldiers moving around upstairs in the house.

One of Prosser's men cried out in fear, "He has the Militia waiting in the house to attack us!"

The man with the deep voice and English accent shouted out in fear, "It is a trap!"

The look on Dr. Prosser's face changed from evil glee to that of someone afraid for his life. He quickly turned and yelled to the others, "Retreat! Retreat!"

Prosser's words were unnecessary because everyone was already running away as fast as they could.

Colonel Ludington was downstairs in the house, peeking out the window. He smiled as he watched Prosser and his men run away. They looked like rats being chased by big invisible angry cats.

He turned and smiled as he looked at, Abigail. She was relieved. She smiled when she saw his smile.

The Colonel proudly called to his children, "You did it children! You did it!" He then shouted a loud, "Huzzah!"

Sybil, Rebecca, Archibald and Henry, Jr. were all excited. They yelled, "Huzzah!" As they did that they realized the other children were still sleeping.

All the noise woke up Derek and Tertullus. They rubbed their eyes, looking half-awake. Derek looked around and said, "Shhh! I am trying to sleep!"

The other children looked at each other, smiled, and then blew out the candles.

Chapter 9

Conflict at the Ganong's Home
March 8, 1777

John Ganong and Jesse his son were splitting wood outside their home on this cold day. Neither one looked happy. They were not talking to each other.

Joseph Angevine, Jesse's friend who belonged to the Militia, quickly rode up to the house. He had some very important news to share with them.

As he drew near, Joseph shouted, "Jesse! Mr. Ganong!"

Jesse and his father stopped splitting wood. They looked up at Joseph. They saw the look of concern on his face. Jesse could tell Joseph came with important news.

Jesse's father, John Ganong, was a successful businessman. His business dealings kept him in close contact with people who had strong Loyalist leanings. Those Loyalists were at odds with the Rebels like Colonel Ludington who backed the Continental cause.

Though John was not an aristocrat he bought many acres of land over the years and built a large home for his family. It was much larger than many others in the area.

Home of Loyalist Beverley Robinson

Many Loyalists in New York were affluent.
Appletons' Cyclopaedia of American Bibliography, 1886

    The Ganong's home was quite a distance away from the simple farm where Joseph lived. Joseph and his father's home was closer to the Ludington's. He rode a long way that morning to get to the Ganong's house.

    Joseph had important news. He could hardly contain himself. He learned how Dr. Prosser and the mob of Loyalists tried to capture Sybil's father . He wanted to let Jesse know what happened.

    Joseph quickly got off his horse. He tied it to one of the fence rails.

    Jesse walked over to Joseph. He shook his hand, and asked, "Joseph, what brings you out here?"

    Joseph was upset as he told what happened, "Jesse! Tories tried to capture Colonel Ludington last night!"

    When Jesse's father heard Joseph say someone tried to capture Colonel Ludington. He was filled with fear and became upset. He was concerned something bad like this was going to happen. Now it did! He tried to warn Colonel Ludington, but he would not listen to him!

John was so upset. He wanted to make sure what he heard was correct. He asked, "Joseph, are you sure?"

Joseph could see John Ganong was troubled.

Joseph shook his head *yes*. He explained slowly and carefully, "Yes, Mr. Ganong, it was Dr. Jonathan Prosser and a large group of Tories!"

John started shaking his head. He spoke out in despair, "This is not good! Not good! I tried to warn Colonel Ludington!"

While Jesse's father was overcome with the idea of things getting worse for himself, Jesse was concerned about the safety of Sybil and the Ludington family.

Jesse asked Joseph, "Did anyone get hurt?"

He saw Joseph perk up a little at that question and get a bit more optimistic.

Joseph was glad to report, "No! The wonderful thing is, no one was hurt."

That was great news to Jesse. A look of relief came over his face. He said, "I am so glad to hear that."

As the news sank in Jesse's look quickly changed to a puzzled one. He asked Joseph, "How could someone try to capture Colonel Ludington, yet no one got hurt?"

Joseph smiled as he explained, "Sybil and her brothers and sisters helped scare them off."

That made Jesse smile, "Sybil and her brothers and sisters helped scare them off?! Why am I not surprised?"

Jesse's father was greatly upset by this whole thing. He could barely think straight. He did not hear Joseph say, *no one was hurt.* All he could think about was how terrible this was and how much worse it could get.

He blamed it all on his stubborn friend, Henry Ludington. He was thinking to himself, *Why would Henry not be reasonable and give up his dangerous conflict with the Crown? Things will only get worse!*

Jesse and Joseph could see John pacing back and forth, and muttering, "This is bad! This is so bad!"

Jesse walked over to his father. He grabbed him by his shoulders, looked him in the eye and said, "Oh Father, can you not see!"

Since the Revolution started Jesse had many conflicts with his father. Jesse believed in the struggle for independence. His father believed the struggle was all a bad misunderstanding.

Jesse previously gave up discussing independence with his father. It always became a heated argument. The Tories attempt to capture Colonel Ludington put his friend's family in danger was too much for him to take. Now, he could no longer contain himself. He had to say something.

Jesse looked straight into father's eyes. He firmly said, "We must take a stand! You cannot be uncommitted!"

He felt this incident might be enough to make his father rethink things.

Hanging of Nathan Hale

*Harper's Weekly, November 24, 1860.
John Ganong knew the Crown hung Rebels.*

Jesse thought this would be a good time to ask his father for something very important to him. He looked at his father and pleaded, "Please let me join the Militia!"

Jesse's father was very upset. He was still shaking his head in disbelief at the news. He knew something bad just happened. He feared much worse would follow if he gave Jesse permission to join the Militia.

He looked back at his son and said, "No! No! Absolutely not!"

That was not what Jesse wanted to hear. He became more upset with his father. He moaned, "Father!"

Jesse's father was extremely upset over what happened. He was afraid his whole world was going to fall apart. He walked away from Jesse muttering, "This is so bad! What are we going to do?"

Joseph knew Jesse was upset and disappointed. He came closer to Jesse. He put his hand on his shoulder and said, "I am so sorry Jesse, if I caused you any trouble."

Jesse responded firmly, "No, Joseph, You, did not cause any trouble!"

He paused a moment then continued, "I love my Father! But he is wrong! He thinks he can sit on the fence and wait this out! He still cannot accept the fact this is a war to the end. I cannot believe he will not open his eyes! Not even after this!"

Jesse's father went into the house shaking his head and muttering.

Jesse looked to where his father was. He said, "I fear this is all going to end badly for people like my father."

Joseph nodded his head in agreement. Then he said, "Yes, I agree. It is time everyone chooses a side and takes a stand."

He walked over to Jesse as he continued to speak, I read that Benjamin Franklin said, *"We must all hang together or assuredly, we will hang separately."*

Jesse nodded his head in agreement. He said, "I am sure the King would like to hang all of us, if he could."

He looked back at the house again as he said. "If only Father would realize that!"

Chapter 10

Sybil's Birthday Party
April 5, 1777

It was April 5, 1777, a beautiful unusually warm spring day in the Hudson Valley. Many friends and family gathered at the home of Colonel Henry Ludington to celebrate the sixteenth birthday of his daughter Sybil.

Sybil, Rebecca, and Mary Ludington were outside enjoying Sybil's party with their friends Joseph Angevine and Jesse Ganong. Some of the younger children were playing *Graces*. That is a colonial game where the children toss a hoop in the air with two sticks. Another child tries to catch it with a second set of two sticks.

Colonel Ludington and Jacob Angevine were talking when two unexpected guests arrived. It was Rev. John Gano and Haym Salomon.

Colonel Ludington knew Gano. He extended his hand, "Rev. John Gano, my favorite *Fighting Preacher*, I am always honored by your presence."

When the Continental Congress formed the Continental Army in 1775, Rev. Gano volunteered. Unlike some other clergy, Gano brought his sword with him and fought alongside the men he served. He earn the nickname *The Fighting Preacher.*

Rev. John Gano

Unknown Artist, 1780's.
New York Public Library

Gano replied, "Colonel Henry Ludington, the honor is always mine."

The Colonel introduced Jacob, "This is my friend Jacob Angevine. He earned his freedom from slavery for his service during the French and Indian War."

Gano shook Jacob's hand warmly. He smiled and said, "It is my pleasure to meet you Jacob."

A very serious look then came across his face. He said, "Slavery is an abomination and should be eradicated from the face of the earth!"

That made Jacob smile. He said, "I wish more men

felt the same as you.

Haym interrupted, "I feel the same way! Slavery is indeed a despicable abomination!

Gano then introduced Haym, "Colonel Ludington, Jacob, I would like to introduce to you my friend, Haym Salomon."

As Haym, Henry and Jacob shook hands, Gano gave some background on Salomon, "Haym came to New York from Poland a few years ago. Soon, after his arrival he became a member of the first synagogue in New York City and a very active member of the Sons of Liberty. He has been a very good friend of the Revolution."

Haym Salomon Silver Medal
1973 Jewish Hall of Fame Medal.

Colonel Ludington smiled, "I am truly honored to meet you Mr. Salomon."

Salomon interrupted, "Please, call me Haym."

The Colonel continued, "Haym, I heard of your efforts to help secure much needed funds to help us finance this war. That funding is so essential to our cause. And, I also heard, as a result of those efforts the Crown arrested you as a spy and let you be their *guest* in one of their jails."

Haym smiled. He humbly replied, "Thank you for your kind words. I am glad to do whatever I can to help the cause of Liberty. And if that means being a *guest* in jail, then that is the price I am willing to pay."

The Colonel was very pleased with Haym's attitude. He patted him on the back and said, "I like you a lot!"

Haym replied, "Colonel Ludington, I understand the Crown would also like to have you as a *guest* in their jail."

The Colonel smiled and said, "Haym, you may call me Henry. And Yes, I know they would like to have me as their *guest*. I hope I keep disappointing them."

"We love to disappoint the Crown," Haym said with a big smile.

Gano explained the reason for their visit, "Haym and I were on our way to meet with the State Assembly at Kingston, when we heard you were having this birthday celebration for your daughter, and Haym asked if we could stop by and see you."

Haym said, "I always enjoy meeting someone who gives the British a hard time."

Henry said, "And I am humbly grateful both of you have honored us with your presence."

Gano looked toward the children playing. He asked Henry, "So, which one is your daughter?"

Henry smiled as he pointed out all four of his daughters. He said, "That one, and that one, and that one, and that one."

Haym smiled when he saw Henry had so many daughters.

Gano smiled. He said, "I meant, which one is the birthday girl?"

Henry pointed to Sybil, "Oh yes, you mean Sybil. That is her, over there." They looked toward Sybil.

Sybil was playing with her friends.

Joseph Angevine said to Sybil, "So Sybil, you are now sixteen years old! You are finally a lady!" He bowed to her and she curtsied back to him.

Rebecca said in jest, "Yes, she is no longer a boy!"

That comment made them all laugh.

Jesse Ganong wanted to be more than just a friend to Sybil. He said, "I am sure no one ever thought that!"

Rebecca smiled and said, "Father does!"

They looked towards their father and all laughed. Henry smiled back at them.

Another set of important guests arrived. Daniel and Abraham Nimham arrived on their horses along with other members of the Wappinger Tribe.

The Nimhams were old friends with the Ludingtons. Daniel Nimham and Henry served together in the French & Indian War. They also opposed the British landlords in the Settler's Revolt.

Daniel and Abraham got off their horses. They greeted Henry with a warm handshake using both hands.

Daniel spoke first, "We could not pass through here without stopping to visit our favorite Englishman."

Henry said, "Daniel, my old friend, I prefer the term

American over *Englishman*."

Daniel said, "I did not mean any offense, my friend."

Sketch of a Stockbridge/Wappinger Indian
*By Captain Johann Ewald, 1798.
Ewald was an officer in the Hessian Army.
He made this image during the Revolution after seeing
Daniel and Abraham Nimham and their men.*

Henry replied, "None was taken."

Henry then made the introductions, "Jacob, you already know these men, but Rev. John Gano, Haym Salomon, I would like to introduce you to my dear friend, Daniel Nimham, Sachem of the Wappinger Indians and his son Abraham."

Gano and Haym started to bow but Daniel and Abraham gave a warm handshake like they gave Henry.

Daniel Nimham, Sachem of the Wappingers
Statue by Michael Keropian, Kent, N.Y.

Haym asked Henry, "Does sachem mean chief?

Henry replied, "Yes, Haym, that is one meaning of the word."

Henry gave them more background of his friendship with Daniel Nimham, "Daniel, Jacob and I served together in the French and Indian War."

Gano spoke to Daniel, "I heard good things about what a great ally you have been in this war, and if I am not mistaken, was it not Beverley Robinson, who is now commander of one of the Loyalist Regiments, the one who used some forged deeds to take away your land, right after you faithfully served the Crown in the French and Indian War?"

Daniel said, "Yes, and Colonel Ludington and many men in this area took up their muskets back then and stood with my people, while I took the fight to the courts and then all the way to England."

Henry said, "Many people do not know the British sent in regiments of Regulars from Poughkeepsie and New York to stop what they called, *The Settler's Revolt*. And it was here that British Regulars fired the first shots against American's. That was five years before the *Boston Massacre*. They tried to keep the whole affair quiet. But, it was that *Revolt* which ignited the spark that helped flame the fires of this Revolution. That *Revolt* caused Samuel Adams to call for the Sons of Liberty to unite!"

Abraham added, "And then, ten years after that, when we heard the English attacked Lexington and Concord. My father and I gathered many of our bravest warriors and went to Boston to join the fight. Hopefully this time we can drive our common enemy off our land!"

They all said, "Here! Here!"

Daniel placed his hand on his son Abraham's shoulder. He then announced, "My son asked General Washington if he could gather all of us Indians into one regiment, to fight the Crown Forces together. And now, I am honored to tell all of you, General Washington granted Abraham's request and combined all Indians into one regiment under Abraham's command."

They all congratulated Abraham with hearty handshakes. Abraham smiled and humbly, but proudly replied, "My father is still the Great Sachem and he is a great and mighty warrior. He is the one who suggested I make the request to General Washington to create the Indian Regiment. Now all Indians will be working together to defeat the British. I only command the regiment because it is my father's wish."

Henry looked at Abraham and said, "I am sure your father and General Washington made a good choice."

Daniel replied, "Yes, my friend, and now we are on our way to New Jersey to help General Washington."

Henry said, "I am so glad you stopped by today. It is excellent timing. Today is my daughter Sybil's sixteenth birthday."

Daniel said, "I remember Sybil as the one who loves horses."

Jacob added, "She was born to ride."

Henry agreed, "She is one of the best riders I know. She is even better than me."

Daniel said, "My son Abraham reminded me about Sybil's birthday. He has a present for her from our family."

Henry smiled, "That is very kind of you."

Abraham asked, "Please excuse me, while I go give Sybil her present."

Abraham went over to Sybil. Sybil was with Rebecca

and their friends. As Abraham approached them Sybil and Rebecca ran to greet him. Joseph and Jesse were concerned at Abraham's warrior-like appearance. They stood back a little.

Sybil smiled and warmly greeted him, "Abraham Nimham! It is so nice to see you again!"

Abraham smiled and said, "Happy Birthday!"

An even bigger smile came across Sybil's face, "That is very kind of you Abraham!"

Abraham reached into his pouch. He pulled out a beaded belt and gave it to Sybil. The Wappinger Tribe, like many other tribes in the Northeast, made belts with beads made from shells for special occasions. This belt was called a wampum belt.

Sybil was very pleased with this special gift. She looked at the belt, "Thank you so much! It is beautiful!"

She noticed two red hearts on the belt. Abraham saw her trace them with her fingers.

He explained, "Those hearts are the symbol of the Nimham family. My grandfather had them on the wampum belt he carried to important councils. The hearts remind us of the importance of approaching others with a true heart. If you do that others will respond with an open heart to you."

Sybil was touched by the gift, "I am so honored."

Abraham smiled. He said, "I understand turning sixteen is a special occasion for your people. If you were one of our people, at this age, this would be more of a wedding gift."

Sybil blushed, and Rebecca giggled at that suggestion.

Abraham looked at Joseph and Jesse with a smile, He said, "Perhaps that belt will help you get a husband."

Sybil blushed even more.

Joseph and Jesse looked at each other when they heard Abraham's words about Sybil finding a husband. They both inwardly liked that idea, but it made them blush. They tried to walk away unnoticed.

As Abraham went back to his father another important guest arrived. Some were glad to see him, many were not. It was Enoch Crosby. He arrived with an extra horse.

When Sybil's father saw Crosby arrive he excused himself and went to greet Crosby.

When Joseph and Jesse saw Crosby, they were disgusted.

Sybil looked at the extra horse with interest.

Joseph spoke with disgust, "Oh, no! That Tory, Enoch Crosby has come to ruin Sybil's party!"

Jesse agreed, "He should know better than to turn up here."

Sybil spoke to them sternly, "Be civil!"

Jesse was angry. He said, "Alright! I will try to keep myself from spitting on him!"

Sybil looked at him with anger.

Joseph noticed Crosby had an extra horse, "Look at that extra horse he has with him, do you think he is going to try to capture the Colonel, so he can claim the bounty?"

Sybil gave Joseph a shove for what he said. Joseph fell

and landed in the dirt on his back.

Enoch Crosby left Sybil's father and came toward Sybil, leading the extra horse.

Jesse helped Joseph up. They stepped away to avoid Crosby.

Crosby came to Sybil. He said, "I have a gift for you Sybil." He offered her the reins to the horse and said, "Happy Birthday!"

Sybil was so excited she could not contain herself. She wanted to make sure she understood what he said. She excitedly asked, "For me?!"

Crosby smiled as he still extended the reins of the horse to Sybil, "Yes, Sybil, it is my birthday gift for you."

The boys gave Crosby a disgusted look.

Jesse looked like he was about to spit at Enoch. Rebecca noticed that. She punched Jesse in the chest so hard he ended up coughing. He looked at Rebecca with a shocked look. She put up two fists threatening him.

Sybil quickly hugged Crosby, accepted the reins, and hugged the horse.

Rebecca glared at Jesse and Joseph. She was letting them know she would not put up with any acts of disrespect from them toward Crosby. She then wiped off her hands and went over to Sybil and the horse.

Rebecca said, "Oh Sybil! What a pretty horse!"

Joseph and Jesse slowly came closer.

Sybil was so happy. She said, "Oh yes! He is the most beautiful horse in the world!"

Rebecca asked, "What are you going to call him?"

Joseph looked at Crosby with disgust and y suggested, "How about King George?"

Rebecca immediately put up her fists again, threatening to hit Joseph, like she did Jesse. She glared at him and said one word, "Joseph!"

Joseph and Jesse wisely stepped back. They did not say another word.

Sybil looked closely at her new horse. She then said, "He looks like a horse that will be good to ride both during the day and at night. At night, when I ride, I always look for the light from the stars to guide me."

She smiled and said, "I am going to call him Star!"

Rebecca replied, "That sounds like a perfect name."

Sybil then turned to Crosby. She said, "Oh thank you so much, Mr. Crosby!"

Jesse and Joseph were especially upset at how respectful Sybil was to Crosby. They looked at Rebecca and knew it was best to be silent.

Sybil's parents, Henry and Abigail came over. Sybil excitedly showed them her new horse, "Oh Father! Mother! This is the best birthday present ever!"

Her parents smiled.

Sybil asked, "Can I take him for a ride?"

Her father said, "It is your horse!"

Sybil quickly jumped up on the horse and rode off.

As she rode off, Crosby pulled Henry aside.

Henry put his hand on Crosby's shoulder as they walked off a little way together. Henry said, "Thank you so much Enoch, I can see Sybil loves her gift."

Crosby smiled, "You are quite welcome. I think that horse will be quite useful one day soon. And, I am so glad you are here to see it and not on some British prison ship."

Henry replied, "So am I, Enoch. It is a good thing Dr. Prosser's plan failed. Thank you for the warning."

Crosby then reminded Henry of another concern, "Henry, remember Dr. Prosser said the British would be coming within the month."

Henry said, "Yes, I hope he is wrong."

Crosby replied, "I do too, but I fear you will be involved in an armed conflict very soon."

Henry replied, "If it must be, we are ready and willing to do our part."

Joseph and Jesse walked by Crosby and Henry and kicked up some dirt.

Henry scolded them, "Lads! Show some respect!"

Jesse answered, "Sorry Colonel Ludington, but when he shows some respect for our country, then maybe we will show him some respect!"

Joseph and Jesse continued to walk off together.

Henry looked at Enoch and said, "Sorry Enoch, you know they mean well."

Crosby smiled. He said, "Yes, I do appreciate their passion and dislike for Tories."

Henry smiled and spoke in jest, "Yes, too bad you are one of those awful Tories."

Henry patted Crosby on the back.

Crosby smiled as he responded, "Yes, it is".

 ## Chapter 11

British Fleet Embarks for Norwalk
New York City
April 22, 1777 – Tuesday 1 p.m.

It was April 22, 1777, a chilly and very windy afternoon. A fleet of twenty-six British ships sat docked at the south end of Manhattan Island. The fleet included war ships, transports, and a hospital ship.

An invasion force of about two thousand soldiers began to board the ships for their raid on the Rebel Supply Depot in Danbury, Connecticut. That force included red-coated British Marines, Regulars from seven different regiments, and mounted dragoons with their tall metallic caps with a fearsome death skull and the words, *Or Glory*. They were joined by Loyalists from General Montfort Browne's Regiment wearing green coats with white facings. Six three-pounder cannons along with artillerymen were also loaded on the ships.

The large force of soldiers tried to quietly board the ships. They hoped to avoid discovery by Rebel spies. The success of this raid depended on the element of surprise.

Earlier in the day a smaller fleet sailed up the Hudson

River. They went north toward Peekskill. There was a direct overland route from Peekskill to Fishkill where the main Rebel Supply Depot was located. They hoped Rebel spies would see the first fleet and think the object of the raid was the Fishkill Supply Depot.

Captain Henry Duncan, commander of the fleet, was standing near the dock supervising the boarding of the fleet for the Danbury Raid.

Governor William Tryon, commander of the invasion force approached Captain Duncan. With him were General James Agnew, General William Erskine, and General Montfort Browne and their aides.

Tryon greeted Duncan with a tip of his hat, "Good afternoon Captain Duncan!"

Duncan returned the salute, "Thank you Governor Tryon."

Tryon introduced the rest of the senior officers, "General James Agnew, General William Erskine, General Montfort Browne, this is Captain Henry Duncan, He will be leading our invasion fleet of twenty-six ships."

Each officer replied with a nod of their head and grabbed the tip of their hats in salute

Erskine complimented Duncan, "Your reputation precedes you Captain Duncan."

Duncan replied, "Thank You, General Erskine."

Tryon signaled to his aides. One aide opened a map while another held the other side. As the other officers gathered around, Tryon pointed at the map, "Captain Duncan and his fleet will take us to this beach, on the east side of Norwalk, Connecticut. It is called Compo Beach. We will be joined there by more of General Browne's local Loyalists. We will then proceed to Danbury."

Erskine asked, "Do we expect much opposition along the way?"

Browne proudly stated, "General Erskine, my Loyalists have informed me the Rebels expect some type of raid, but just as we hoped, they fortified their depot at Fishkill thinking that is the target and they have only left a token force at Danbury!"

Erskine asked another question, "And what of Norwalk? Do we expect much resistance there?"

Tryon said, "It is my understanding they do not suspect a thing. When they see Captain Duncan's fleet arrive and see General Browne's Loyalists assemble. I am sure their hearts will turn cold and they will run rather than fight!"

Browne proudly said, "My men and I do have that kind of effect!"

Tryon and Erskine looked at each other, obviously upset with Browne's prideful comment.

While they were talking, Duncan saw the last of the soldiers board the ships. With that task completed he announced, "Gentlemen, your fleet awaits you!

The generals boarded their ships. Sailors withdrew the boarding ramps. Others untied the docking ropes. The ships opened their uppermost sails. The blowing wind quickly filled the sails, allowing them the ships to sail away.

They did not realize they were about to quickly end up in bad weather . It would toss their ships around in the waters surrounding Manhattan for three days.

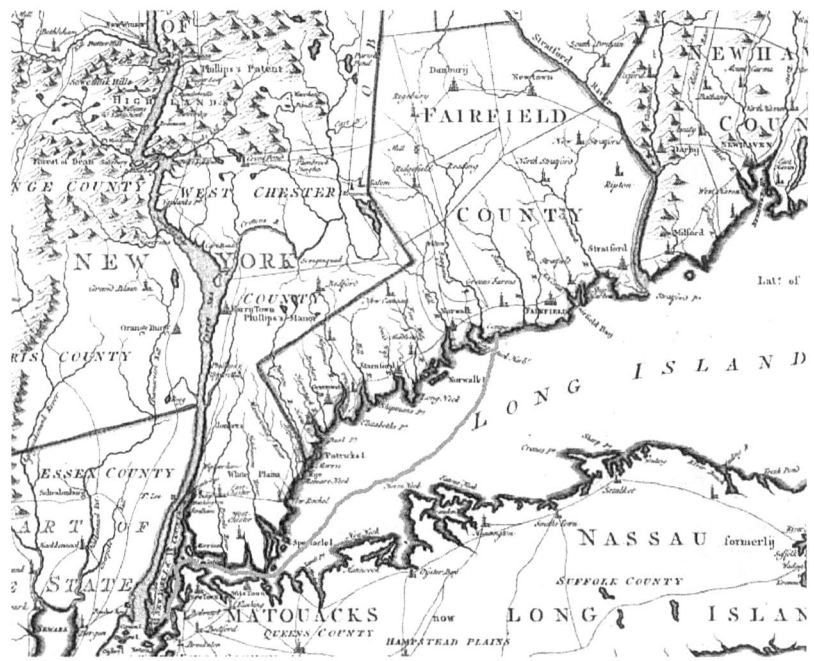

The Route the British Fleet Took to Compo Beach

Engraving by Covens and Mortier, 1780
The fleet left Lower Manhattan on Tuesday, April 22, 1777.
Bad Weather caused long delays.
One of the ships became stuck on rocks yet finally sailed through the narrow channel and into Long Island Sound.
They did not arrive at Compo Beach until Friday, April 25, 1777.

Chapter 12

Shooting Muskets

April 25, 1777 – Friday Morning

The morning of April 25, 1777 started out as a cold, dreary spring day in the Hudson Valley of New York and in neighboring Connecticut. The Rebels were expecting the Crown Forces to attack one of their supply depots within the month. They were unaware a fleet of twenty-seven British ships, loaded with troops, was on its way to Norwalk, Connecticut, to launch a raid against the Rebel Supply Depot in Danbury. The British Commander General, The Lord William Howe, believed this raid could bring an end to the Revolution.

It was a quiet morning, until the silence was broken by the loud sound of a blast from a musket. That blast was followed by the sound of footsteps, running through the woods. The sound of footsteps stopped briefly. The silence was shattered again by another loud musket blast.

It was not one of the soldiers from the invading force who fired the musket. It was seventeen-year old Joseph Angevine, a member of the Dutchess County Militia. He was not shooting at the enemy. He was practicing shooting a musket with his friend, Sybil Ludington.

A lot of musket practice was done standing still. Joseph knew that would not be enough to prepare him for the coming conflict. That is why he practiced running and shooting.

After he finished running through the woods and shooting the musket a second time, Sybil came towards him and said, "Not bad, Joseph."

Joseph was tired and breathing heavily. He knew Sybil was very familiar with the Militia drill and was good with a musket. He was pleased with her compliment. He looked at Sybil and said, "Thank you."

Sybil gave him a big smile and said, "A bit more practice and you may almost be as good as me!"

Joseph was not sure if Sybil was teasing him.

Suddenly, they heard someone on horseback coming their way. They looked around cautiously. They were relieved when they saw it was their friend, Jesse Ganong.

Sybil called out, "Over here, Jesse!"

Jesse heard the musket blasts, as he was approaching. He had an idea it was Sybil and Joseph. He headed directly over to them.

As Jesse came close, Joseph gave him a warm greeting, "Jesse, it is good to see you!"

Joseph shifted the musket to his left hand and reached up and shook Jesse's hand.

Jesse smiled as he replied, "Joseph!"

Jesse got off his horse and bowed his head to Sybil. He said, "Sybil!" She replied giving him a small curtsey.

Jesse looked at the musket Joseph was holding. He asked, "Can I have a turn with that?"

Joseph looked at Jesse with surprise. He knew Jesse never fired a musket because his father would not let him join the Militia. Joseph asked him, "Are you sure?"

Jesse looked back at him and said, "Very sure!"

Joseph and Sybil looked at each other and smiled. Joseph handed Sybil the musket to hold. He then took off the cartridge box and handed it to Jesse. Jesse put it on. Sybil then handed Jesse the musket.

Jesse looked at the musket, "So, how do I do this?"

As Joseph reached slowly for the musket to show him. Sybil grabbed it back out of Jesse's hands,

Joseph stepped back with a smile on his face. He watched Sybil take charge.

Sybil reached into the cartridge box, which Jesse was wearing. She removed a cartridge. She then demonstrated the way to load the musket step by step.

Sybil held the musket in her left hand with the lock facing towards Jesse and said, "First, you open the pan like this."

She opened the pan on the musket with her right hand, "Then, you prime the pan."

Sybil bite off the end of the cartridge. She spit out the end and put some powder in the pan.

"Then, you close the pan, cast about and load the charge." Sybil cast the musket about and put the rest of the cartridge in the end of the barrel.

"Then, you ram the charge." She pulled out the

rammer and pushed the charge down the barrel in one swoop.

"You then, return the rammer." Sybil pulled the ramrod from the barrel and put it back in its channel.

"Then, you come to the poise." She placed the musket in front of her face.

"You then, make ready." Sybil said, as she cocked the musket, while in the *poise* position.

"Then, Present." She then pointed the musket at the woods.

"And then, Fire!" Sybil pulled the trigger and the musket shot with a blast! The bullet flew into the woods and hit something.

Joseph smiled as he saw how smoothly Sybil did the loading and firing. Jesse watched paying close attention.

Sybil handed Jesse the musket, "Now Jesse, you do it."

Jesse accepted the musket. He then looked at Joseph, indicating he needed help. He did not want to say that. Joseph smiled, nodded, and pointed toward Sybil.

Jesse then looked at Sybil. She smiled, nodded her head, and then gave the commands.

First, she said, "Prime and load!"

Jesse looked like he did not understand. Joseph explained, "That means to grab a cartridge and follow the loading and firing commands."

Jesse grabbed a cartridge from the cartridge box.

Sybil continued with the orders, "Open, pan!"

Jesse opened the pan.

Sybil gave the next command, "Prime the pan!"

Jesse bite off the end of the cartridge. He spit it out and slowly poured some powder in the pan.

Sybil interrupted him. She did not want him to put in too much powder, "That is enough!"

Jesse stopped. Then Sybil continued the orders, "Close pan, cast about, and charge the barrel."

Jesse almost hit himself in the head as he cast the musket about.

Joseph smiled and put his hand over his mouth trying not to laugh. Sybil also smiled.

Jesse put the cartridge down the barrel.

Sybil continued the orders, "Ram the charge!"

Jesse withdrew the rammer wildly, almost hitting himself. Joseph laughed. Sybil tried to act serious but could not help but smile.

Jesse rammed the charge down the barrel.

Sybil continued the orders, "Return, rammer!"

Jesse fumbled to return the ramrod. He finally got it back in the channel.

Sybil spoke, "Come to the poise!"

Jesse did not understand.

Joseph motioned to Jesse to put the musket in front of his face.

Jesse raised the musket in front of his face, but not correctly.

Sybil helped him get the musket in the proper position.

Then she said, "Make ready!"

Jesse cocked the musket in the *Poise* position.

Sybil gave the command, "Present!"

Jesse pointed the musket into the woods.

Sybil stopped. She gave Jesse one last word of advice, "Make sure you exhale as you pull the trigger."

Jesse nodded his head. Then Sybil gave the last command, "Fire!"

Jesse closed his eyes and fired. As the musket fired it threw him a little off balance.

Sybil yelled at him, "Next time, plant your feet better. And never close your eyes when you shoot!"

Joseph was watching and smiling the whole time.

Jesse smiled and jokingly responded, "Yes! Sergeant!"

Sybil looked at him very seriously, "Wipe that smile off your face, soldier!"

She then started to laugh. Then they all laughed.

Then Sybil got very serious and said, "Try that again. And this time, imagine you are shooting a Tory!"

Jesse nodded his head. Something seemed to click. His got a very serious look. He replied, "Yes! Sergeant!"

This time, as Sybil gave the commands, Jesse did it all smoothly.

Sybil gave the first command, "Prime and load!"

Jesse put the musket in the position to load. He quickly grabbed a cartridge from the cartridge box.

She gave the next command, "Open, pan!"

Jesse smoothly opened the pan.

Sybil continued, "Prime the pan!"

Jesse bit off the end of the cartridge. He spit it out and put the right amount of powder in the pan.

Sybil gave the next command, "Close the pan, cast about and charge the barrel!"

Jesse closed the pan. He cast the musket about and put the cartridge down the barrel.

Sybil continued, "Ram the charge!"

Jesse withdrew the rammer in one swift motion and rammed the charge down the barrel.

Sybil gave the next order, "Return, rammer!

Jesse quickly returned the ramrod.

Sybil said, "Come to the poise!"

Jesse raised the musket in front of his face in the proper position. He looked like a true veteran.

Sybil continued, "Make ready!"

Jesse cocked back the hammer on the musket.

Sybil said, "Present!"

Jesse pointed the musket into the woods.

Sybil gave the final command, "Fire!"

Jesse fired the musket smoothly. There was a blast and a brief controlled kickback from the musket.

Joseph was impressed. He came over, patted Jesse on the back. He said, "Well done, Jesse!"

Sybil came close and congratulated Jesse. She gave him a kiss on the cheek as she said, "Well done!"

Jesse blushed at the kiss. Joseph looked startled.

Just as they finished, it then started to rain.

Loading a Musket

Franklyn Maxwell, 4th New York Regiment of the Continental Line, loading a Musket in Patterson (Fredericksburg), New York.
Photograph by Larry A. Maxwell

 ## Chapter 13

Crown Forces Land at Norwalk
April 25, 1777 – Friday 5 p.m.

The British invasion force of two thousand men landed at Compo Beach, near Norwalk, Connecticut. It was about five o'clock on the rainy afternoon of Friday, April 25, 1777. They planned to march to Danbury and destroy the Rebel Supply Depot. They hoped that would bring a swift end to the Rebellion.

They left New York City three days before, on the afternoon of Tuesday April 22. They hoped to arrive at Compo Beach that evening undetected.

Things did not go as planned. It took them three days longer to get to Compo Beach than they expected. When they attempted to leave New York City they faced unexpected strong winds. The winds kept changing directions and even trapped one of the ships at one point.

Those winds, which preceded two days of rain, kept blowing the fleet in the opposite direction. It took Captain Henry Duncan's experience and excellent navigational skills to get the fleet out of the East River, into Long Island Sound, and over to Norwalk.

Compo Beach at Low Tide

Late Afternoon – The time of day the Crown Forces landed.
Photograph by Larry A. Maxwell, 2017

Compo Beach at Sunset

Crown Forces unloaded until 10 o'clock at night.
Photograph by Larry A. Maxwell, 2017

Compo Beach was not a harbor with docks for war ships. The generals and their army had to go to shore from their large ships on smaller landing craft.

When they landed, as the rest of the troops began the long process of unloading and coming ashore, the generals gathered together to discuss their plans.

Governor Tryon said to Captain Duncan, "Captain Duncan, I must commend you. I never expected such contrary winds when we set out. Yet you handled the fleet quite well."

Duncan nodded his head in thanks for the compliment, "Thank you Governor Tryon. I never had such a challenge as I did in those waters. I apologize for the delay."

Tyron replied, "I am not happy about the delay but there is no apology necessary Captain. You have no control over the weather. You did your job very well and gave us a safe voyage the rest of the way."

Erskine changed the subject. He was eager to begin the attack, "It is time to teach the Rebels a lesson!"

As the rest of the troops were unloading a company of Loyalists arrived from the surrounding area. They were part of General Montfort Browne's Prince of Wales Loyalist Regiment. They brought along some new recruits who joined when they heard there was a chance this action would help bring a swift end to the Rebellion.

The sight of the British fleet and the company of armed Loyalists along the shore helped discourage resistance from the local town folk in Norwalk.

The leader of the local Loyalist Company came to the

group of officers. He was looking for General Browne, his commander.

He took off his hat and bowed his head in in salute, "General Browne, we are at your service."

Crown Forces Landing at Compo Beach
By Robert Lynn Lambdin
Westport Schools Permanent Art Collection
On Display at Westport Town Hall

Browne smiled as he saw the company of Loyalists in their green uniforms along with the group of new recruits.

He returned the salute with a nod of his hat. He said to the leader of the Loyalist Company, "Thank you son. Have your company join the rest of the regiment!"

The Loyalist officer replied, "Yes, Sir!"

He rejoined his company and had them march off to join the rest of General Montfort Browne's Regiment.

Browne looked at the others and proudly said, "With my Loyal Regiment, I am sure we will have the victory."

Tryon and Erskine looked at each other, obviously tired of Browne's proudful attitude.

Tryon spoke in jest, "Perhaps General Agnew, General Erskine and I should wait here with our regiments while you and your Loyalists take care of the Rebels?"

Browne did not catch the fact Tryon was joking. He replied like he thought it was a good suggestion but then realized that probably was not the best idea.

He said to Tryon, "I would hate to have you come all this way and not get a chance to see my men and I in action."

Tryon was not pleased with Browne's response.

Erskine was upset. He said, "Governor Browne (he said *Governor* instead of using *General*, Browne's preferred title) you egotistical, pompous bag of wind! Perhaps I should remind you, Governor Tryon is the one in charge!"

Browne was shocked at Erskine's words.

Erskine continued, "And never forget, your *Loyalists* never did enlist in a Regular unit, but waited to see how things would turn out before they joined us."

Browne did not like Erskine's comments.

Erskine said more, "And we are not even sure if we can really trust them, so we gave them those green regimentals instead of red ones, so we can easily distinguish them from the faithful Regular troops!"

Browne was greatly insulted. He replied, "Well, I never!"

Tryon said, "Gentlemen! Gentlemen! Let us remember who the real enemy is!"

Browne turned away in a huff and headed over to his troops.

Tryon smiled at Erskine. He nodded his head, and said, "And, General Erskine."

Erskine looked at Tryon.

Tryon smiled and leaned closer to Erskine. He said, somewhat quieter, "Well said."

Erskine smiled, then headed to join his troops.

It was getting late in the day. It took four hours to get all the men off the boats. There was no time to set up camp and rest. They needed to march the entire way to Danbury, in the rain, so they could catch the Rebels unaware.

To mislead the Rebels from their destination they choose to first march east towards Fairfield instead of marching directly north to Danbury.

Chapter 14

Conflict Between Father and Son
April 25, 1777 – Late Friday Afternoon

It was late in the afternoon on Friday, April 25, 1777. John Ganong was seated in his home reading while his wife Mary was doing some needlework. They had no idea the Crown Forces were landing at Compo Beach.

John was a successful businessman. Though he did not consider himself a Loyalist he had many business associates with strong Loyalist ties. That helped his business succeed. The success of his business allowed him to build a home which was larger and more comfortable than most of his neighbors.

The silence was disturbed as the door opened and John's son Jesse entered. He was wet from riding in the rain. The rain started when he finished his musket practice with his friends Sybil and Joseph. He entered the house and started to walk right past his father. He was angry with his father. It showed on his face.

John asked, "Jesse, where have you been?"

Jesse planned to walk right past his father. When his father spoke to him, he stopped. He stood still looking ahead, not making eye contact. He replied, "I have been with Sybil and Joseph."

Jesse's father knew Sybil was Colonel Henry Ludington's daughter. He also knew Joseph was in the Militia. He feared it would only bring more trouble to his family if Joseph continued to be with them.

John looked closely at his son Jesse. He thought he noticed something on his face. He stood up and went over to Jesse to get a closer look. He saw some black powder from shooting a musket on Jesse's face. He also recognized a familiar odor. Having served in the French and Indian War he knew the smell of the black powder left upon a person after firing a musket.

He was upset at what he saw and smelled. In an angry tone he said, "You smell like black powder!"

Jesse responded with a shrug and started to walk away. After the Loyalists attempted to capture Colonel Ludington, and his father refused to allow him to join the militia, Jesse no longer cared what his father thought.

As Jesse walked away, John spoke again. Jesse stopped and listened with his back to his father. "Son, you must realize this Rebellion is a lost cause. It is going to end soon."

His father tried to add something he thought was positive, "We will have peace again. The King and Parliament mean good for us. They will not harm us if we just leave them alone!"

Jesse turned around and looked angrily at his father. He disagreed with everything his father just said. He said,

"Father! They will not leave us alone! The King and Parliament would rather have us all hanged, than have peace!"

Jesse looked his father directly in the eye and said, "When will you realize we are at war! If we do not fight for our liberty what are we worth?"

Jesse then stormed off.

John was cut to the heart by his son's words. He shook his head then put his head in his hands.

His wife sat by silently during this conflict. She did not like seeing her husband and son at odds with each other. She feared something bad would come from this.

Tory Tax Collector

*Some Loyalists were abused by Rebel mobs.
Nicolas Ponce and Francois Godefroy, engraving circa 1784.*

 ## Chapter 15

Confrontation at Bethel
April 26, 1777 – Saturday Afternoon

It was Saturday afternoon, April 26, 1777. The Crown Forces left Compo Beach about ten o'clock last night. The steady rain made the roads very muddy. That made it very hard moving their six cannons. They were also slowed down by some small resistance on the way. They were glad when they reached Redding about eleven o'clock in the morning. They took a two-hour break for breakfast.

Before the Crown Forces arrived many people who sided with the Rebel cause fearfully loaded wagons and headed out of town. Those who remained saw no hope offering resistance. The Loyalists enjoyed rounding up their Rebel neighbors and taking prisoners.

About one o'clock in the afternoon General William Erskine led them out of town. The Crown Forces resumed their march. They continued north toward Bethel. Their destination was the supply depot at Danbury.

When they came to Hoyt's Hill in Bethel, part of Danbury, a rider appeared at the top of the hill in front of them. He was riding a horse and horse waving a sword over his head like a general in command of an army.

General Erskine, who was leading the Crown Forces, was alarmed when he saw the figure waving his sword. It looked like a general preparing his men for an attack. Erskine was not going to allow his men to fall into a trap.

He yelled the command, "Come to the halt." The whole army abruptly stopped.

Erskine watched and listened. The figure on the hill turned to look back over his shoulder. He then yelled, "Halt! The whole universe! Break off by nations!"

Erskine was puzzled, He never heard such commands before. It sounded like there must be a very large force waiting to oppose them over the crest of that hill.

General William Tryon rode to the front to see why the advance stopped. General Agnew and General Browne stayed back with their troops. General Erskine updated Tryon, who then took command.

Rather than change head-on into an unknown force Tryon decided to make a stand. He pulled out his sword. He then yelled, "Advance the cannons to the front!"

His command was echoed by other officers down the line, "Advance the cannons to the front!"

The two long columns of soldiers moved to each side of the road to allow the artillery crews to trudge ahead. They struggled to move the cannons up the muddy road. Each cannon created ruts in the road. That made it more difficult to move the other cannons.

Finally, all six cannons were in front of the army

spread out in a wide row ready to stop the enemy attack.

The officer on the hill, ahead of them, rode back and forth holding his sword straight up in the air. He looked at the Crown Forces with a fierce glare.

When the cannons were in place Governor Tryon called out, "From column into line!"

Crown Forces Wait for the Enemy to Attack
Crown Forces reenactors waiting for orders to attack.
Photograph by Gary Vorwald

Officers echoed, "From column into line."

The Crown Forces formed neat orderly rows between and behind the artillery.

As the troops were forming rows, Governor Tryon yelled, "Load cannons!"

Each of the artillery captains gave the orders to their crews to prepare and load each cannon.

As the cannons were loading, Tryon yelled orders to the soldiers lined up in rows, "Prime and Load!"

The officers echoed his command, "Prime and Load!"

Every man loaded their muskets. Then they held in the *ready* position in front of their faces.

All eyes were looking at the summit. They watched with concern as the officer on the hill rode back over the summit and out of sight. They had no idea how great a force opposed them or what lay ahead.

Everyone waited with concern. They expected the front line of the Rebel Army to advance over the hill.

They waited and waited. Then waited some more.

General Erskine stood firmly on his horse, next to Governor Tryon, with his sword draw.

Tryon noticed the long wait made some of his men started to move nervously. He yelled, "Steady!"

The other officers echoed his command, "Steady!"

After what seemed a long while Erskine looked at Tryon and asked, "Do you think they are waiting for us to advance on them?"

"They must think me a fool if they think I will charge blindly over a hill!" Tryon replied adamantly.

"Neither would I," Erskine agreed.

Tryon said, "We shall wait for them to advance and then we will crush them!"

Erskine agreed that was the best strategy, "Well said!"

As they waited for the Rebel advance General Browne wondered what was delaying the action. He finally came riding up to join Tryon and Erskine.

He asked, "What are we waiting for?"

Erskine was impatient with Browne. He angrily replied, "We are waiting for them to attack us! We are not foolish enough to ride over the hill into an ambush!"

Browne did not like Erskine's attitude. He looked at Tryon and said, "Perhaps I should send some of my scouts around their flank to assess the size of their army?"

Tryon was tired of waiting. He liked that idea and replied, "Excellent idea General Browne! Send out your scouts!"

Browne gave Erskine a proud look as he replied to Tryon, "Yes! Sir!" He then rode back to his men.

In a few moments three scouts on horseback headed to the left of the summit. Three headed to the right.

Tryon, Erskine, and the rest of the army watched and waited.

The scouts came riding back over the hill much sooner than expected. That surprised everyone.

The first scout back yelled, "There is no one there!"

Tryon and Erskine sat on their horses in disbelief as the other scouts reported the same thing.

General Browne rode back to the front to hear the report.

Erskine smiled, "They must have run away like scared rabbits when they saw the size of our force!"

Tryon asked the scouts, "Could you tell how many of them there were as they retreated?"

The scouts all replied, "One."

Erskine asked, "One regiment?"

One of the scouts replied, "No, Sir. All we saw was one rider riding away as fast as he could."

What the scouts saw was twenty-five-year-old Luther Holcomb riding off by himself. Holcomb smiled a big smile as he rode off knowing his plan worked. He single-handedly delayed the entire army of the Crown Forces.

General Browne could not contain himself. He laughed and said to Erskine, "No, we are not foolish!"

1796 German Map of Connecticut

Bethel is Northeast of Danbury.
Printed by Sotzsen, Hamburg, Germany

Chapter 16

Danbury Attacked

April 26, 1777 – Late Saturday Afternoon

After marching all day and night through the rain for almost thirty miles, the Crown Forces finally reached Danbury. It was late in the afternoon on Saturday, April 26, 1777. They only had two hours of rest at Redding and survived facing Luther Holcomb and his invisible army. They were tired but liked the thought of destroying the Rebel supplies and ending the Rebellion.

Governor William Tryon, General James Agnew and General William Erskine gathered outside of Danbury.

Governor Tryon spoke, "Gentlemen, we made it to Danbury without much opposition."

General Montfort Browne sent his scouts ahead to see what type of resistance they would face in Danbury. He was very pleased with the word he received back from them. He joined the other officers. He greeted Tryon and Agnew. He purposefully did not greet Erskine.

Tryon asked, "General Browne! What news do you bring?"

He gave his report with an *I told you so* attitude. He

was proud he was correct that they would make it to Danbury without much *real* opposition.

Browne could not forget Erskine's negative comments. He was gloating over the incident in Bethel. He sneered at Erskine as he gave his report. "It is exactly as I said! The Rebels thought we planned to attack Fishkill. So, all they left here is a small token force defending Danbury."

Erskine was glad to hear the good report but did not like Browne's attitude.

Tryon looked at his officers and said, "Gentlemen, you have your orders. It is time to teach the Rebels a lesson which they will not forget. Let us see how well their little Rebellion goes without their supplies!"

He then said, "Take what you can and burn the rest!"

Tryon looked at Browne, "Make sure your Loyalists tie a ribbon on their doors, so their homes will be protected!"

Browne shook his head in agreement and responded, "We shall protect our Loyalists and destroy the Rebels!"

Tryon said, "Long live the King!"

The others all said, "Long live the King!"

Then they rode to join their soldiers.

This was the second day a cold spring rain fell. It was heavy at times. Everything and everyone was soaked. Battles were not usually fought in the rain. Muskets will not fire if the black powder gets wet. That is why soldiers were exhorted to *keep their powder dry*. Despite the rain the generals leading the raid knew they had to follow through with the attack. If the muskets would not fire they knew they could use their bayonets.

General Erskine led the first Brigade into town at about 5 p.m. As he did the rain began to slow down.

Colonel Joseph Platt Cooke
Portrait by William Jennys, 1790-1795

Colonel Joseph Platt Cooke was Commander of the Rebel Supply Depot at Danbury. Earlier in the day he received an appeal from General Silliman to send troops to the coast to help repel an invasion by the Crown Forces. General Silliman did not know the Supply Depot at Danbury was the Crown Forces destination. Colonel Cooke sent some Militia along with most of the men from the 1st Connecticut Regiment, under the command of Colonel Jedediah Huntington. That left only one hundred men with Colonel Cooke to defend Danbury.

Colonel Cooke stood with his men on the main street with his sword drawn waiting for the Crown Forces.

Thomas Starr stood next to him. He was bravely holding the Liberty flag. The Liberty flag was used as a battle flag throughout the Revolution. It's thirteen-alternating red and white stripes waved boldly.

From the time they landed at Compo until they reached Danbury the Crown Forces tried to be as quiet as possible. Now there was no need to be quiet. They marched into town with drummers and fifers playing.

Musicians Play as Crown Forces Enter Town
Gary Vorwald and musicians lead troops into battle.
Photo by Kenneth Grant

As the powerful sound of the music drew closer, Colonel Cooke yelled to his men, "Form a line here!"

Cooke's men quickly formed a line with two rows. They were concerned but ready to do whatever they could to stop the advance of the enemy.

Cooke then yelled to his men, "Prime and load!"

Cooke's men bravely loaded their muskets. Then they stood waiting for the arrival of the Crown Forces.

Soon two Continental soldiers came running down the road as fast as they could. One of them cried out, "Colonel Cooke they are almost here!"

The Crown Forces appeared with an overwhelming number of soldiers. They were coming down the street in a slow determined march. General Erskine was leading the advance on horseback as the musicians played.

As more and more Crown Forces arrived the situation began to look more desperate to Cooke and his men.

Erskine was startled when he saw Cooke's men standing in the street. The thing that startled him was the fact Cooke's men were wearing red regimental coats faced in white. In the British Army, only royal regiments wore red coats faced in white. It appeared to him they were facing British Regulars.

Erskine was an officer and a gentleman. He would never shoot someone unless he was positive they were the enemy. He ordered his men to stop.

The Crown Forces came to a sudden halt. Erskine lowered his sword. His men stood in line with their muskets on their left shoulders.

Colonel Cooke was pleased to see the Crown Forces stop. He wondered how long that would last.

Erskine did not know he was facing the local Militia and some men from the 1st Connecticut Regiment of the Continental Line. The men in the 1st Connecticut Regiment wore red coats faced in white. That was their traditional uniform from before the Revolution. Colonel Cooke also wore a red coat faced white.

Erskine was puzzled when he saw the Liberty flag. He had seen those flags in battle and knew it was a symbol of the Rebellion.

The Liberty Flag
Don Hewitt, 1932 Postcard.

General Browne rode up to Erskine. He wanted to attack. He asked Erskine, "Why have we stopped?"

Erskine explained, "It looks like there are some of our Regulars standing over there in the street!" He pointed down the street and added, "But they are flying the accursed Liberty flag, the battle flag of the Rebels!"

Browne was surprised to see the red coats. He had heard about the Liberty flag. He knew if those men were holding a symbol of the Rebellion then this was not good. He said, "If that flag is the Rebel's battle flag I do not care what they are wearing they are traitors."

Erskine replied, "Seeing those red coats with white facings made me stop. As you know those white facings usually indicate royal regiments from England or Wales and I do not want to fire on our own men. But I agree, that flag is clearly an unacceptable symbol and cannot be tolerated."

Erskine turned to Browne and said, "Go back and get your men ready for action."

Browne smiled and replied, "My men and I are always ready to take action against the Rebel scum."

Erskine raised his sword and yelled the commands to his men, "First Company! Make Ready! Present! Fire!"

They pointed their muskets at the Rebels and fired. It felt like the ground shook as the sound of a massive volley of muskets filled the air. The musket balls stuck some Rebels. They fell helplessly to the ground.

Colonel Cooke quickly replied. He yelled the firing commands to his men, "Make Ready! Present! Fire!"

As Cooke's men fired, two soldiers next to General Erskine were struck and killed. Erskine was shaken but shouted to his men, "Prime and Load!"

The Crown Forces loaded their muskets again.

As the Crown Forces reloaded, Cooke yelled to his men, "Fire at will!"

Cooke's men, though greatly outnumbered, stood bravely. They reloaded and continued firing. As soon as each man shot his musket he loaded it, fired it again, and then reloaded and fired again.

When the Crown Forces completed loading, Erskine yelled, "Fix! Bayonets!"

The soldiers put their bayonets on the end of their muskets. That allowed them to either fire or use the bayonets in a bayonet charge. That action struck fear in the heart of Cooke's men.

Cooke realized his men could not withstand a British bayonet charge. He yelled to his men, "Retreat! Retreat!"

Cooke and his men withdrew. Those who were loaded, shot at the Crown Forces, then turned and ran.

Erskine yelled, "Bayonet Charge! Advance!"

The Crown Forces yelled *Huzzah* and went forward in a smooth, powerful line.

The Regulars were followed by Loyalists who went into buildings looking for Rebel supplies. When they came to a house, they looked to see if there was a ribbon tied to the door. If there was a ribbon they turned away.

Muskets continued to fire. People were yelling and screaming in fear. Loyalists continued looting, taking supplies out of shops and homes.

Some Loyalists came out of one building rolling crates of rum out into the street. They yelled *"Huzzah!"* as they opened some of the crates and loudly laughed with glee as they filled mugs with rum and passed them around.

Some of the Regulars looked around to make sure an officer was not watching, then joined in the drinking.

Carts were seized and loaded with the stolen supplies. When a building was emptied, it was set aflame. Once the carts were filled, the extra supplies were piled in the street and set on fire.

Colonel Cooke stopped behind a building and spoke with messengers getting on their horses. He said, "Go to the colonels of the local Militias and tell them the Regulars and Tories have attacked and are burning Danbury!"

As the messengers rode away, the Crown Forces pressed towards Cooke and his men. Cooke's' men fired their muskets back at the Crown Forces.

Cooke yelled, "Retreat!" They turned and followed him heading away from the Crown Forces.

Musket fire continued. People were screaming all around Danbury. The Crown Forces took some away at gunpoint as the looting and burning continued.

The rain that slowed earlier started to fall again.

Larry A. Maxwell

Danbury Raid Monument

Plaque on a Boulder on Main Street, Danbury, Connecticut. Remembering the Danbury Raid. It reads: *The Revolutionary Village Which Centered About This Green With Its Store Of Supplies For The Army Was Sacked And Burned By A Force Of Two Thousand British April 26, 1777 Warned Of The Gathering Militia The Raiders Departed Next Morning In Haste But Were Attacked And Harassed By The Rising Colonials And Driven To The Refuge Of Their Boats On The Sound*
They Kindled A Fire That Blazed At Saratoga
Photograph by Larry A. Maxwell, 2018

Chapter 17

American Officers Meet at Redding

April 26, 1777 – Late Saturday Afternoon

It was late afternoon on Saturday, April 26, 1777. General Silliman and almost four hundred Militia were almost at Redding, Connecticut. Rain fell for the past two days soaking everyone. The Crown Forces left Redding a few hours ago, reached Danbury and began their raid.

General Silliman lived in Fairfield, Connecticut, not far from where the Crown Forces landed. He received word of the landing early Saturday before sunrise. He sent word to the Militia in Connecticut. and as far away as Massachusetts, calling for help to repel the invasion.

To mislead the Rebels and disguise their destination, the Crown Forces marched east toward Fairfield instead of directly north toward Danbury.

Silliman sent a message to Colonel Joseph Platt Cooke at Danbury to send as many men as possible to help him. Colonel Cooke sent most of his force. Silliman did not yet know Danbury was the Crown Forces destination or he would not have given that order.

Silliman's scouts reported Governor Tryon and his

army turned north and headed toward Redding. Silliman sent messengers to inform others. Then he led his men toward Redding to try to stop the Crown Forces.

When Silliman was about two miles south of Redding there was a break in the rain. Another general approached on horseback leading a small group of men.

Silliman was pleased when he recognized this general as one many people respected. Silliman knew that officer's battlefield experience could be a big help.

When that general drew near to Silliman, he grabbed the edge of his hat and nodded. That was the kind of salute given to one of equal or lower status.

That general said, "General Silliman, I was visiting family and came as soon as I received the news about the Crown Forces invasion and your request to meet you at Redding."

Silliman greeted him with greater respect. Instead of touching the brim of his hat, Silliman took off his hat which was much more respectful and nodded his head in salute as he said, "General Benedict Arnold it is a pleasure to see you again."

At that time General Benedict Arnold was a well-respected general. He was considered a hero of the Revolution. Later his heroism would be forgotten by most when he becomes America's most notorious traitor.

Silliman continued his very respectful greeting, "General Arnold, I am honored by your presence and can most assuredly use your assistance." Arnold smiled appreciating and replied, "I appreciate those kind words.

I understand this engagement falls under the authority of the State of Connecticut. Seeing your commission comes from the State of Connecticut and mine from the Continental Congress, I humbly submit myself to you. I will have my men fall in with yours and we can head to Redding together."

Portrait of General Benedict Arnold

A miniature by Pierre Eugene Du Simitiere, October 3, 1780
This is considered the only authentic portrait of Benedict Arnold.

Arnold loved to be in charge but understood this action was under the authority of Connecticut. That meant General Silliman outranked him. That is the only reason he offered fall in under General Silliman.

Silliman and Arnold then rode together to Redding. Their combined force of soldiers followed them.

When they arrived in town they were directed to the home of a member of the Militia who escaped capture by the Crown Forces. He told them the Crown Forces arrived with around two thousand men and six cannons. He said that they stopped for lunch, took some prisoners, and left only a few hours before the Rebels arrived.

Shortly after Silliman and Arnold arrived Major General David Wooster entered town. He came with another hundred men. He was sent to the home where Silliman and Arnold were located.

Wooster was older than Arnold. When he arrived, Arnold greeted him with proper respect. He removed his hat and make a small bow as he respectfully said, "General David Wooster."

Instead of returning the salute Wooster extended his hand and gave Arnold a handshake. He said, "General Benedict Arnold, I am so glad you are here. I am sure your experience will be a great help to us!"

Wooster then turned to Silliman, took off his hat and nodded his head in salute as he said, "General Silliman it is an honor to fall in with you."

Silliman returned the same hat-off salute and replied, "General Wooster, I am honored to have you here and humbly turn command over to you."

Arnold accepted Wooster's command. He said,

"General Wooster, how may I best serve?"

Silliman said, "Our host informed us the Crown Forces left here marching north to Bethel. They have a force of close to two thousand men along with six cannons."

Portrait of General David Wooster

This portrait is attributed to J. B. Longacre, published in 1835. This bears a strong resemblance to the fictitious Thomas Hart portraits of 1776. It also looks very similar to Richard Purcell's portrait of Lord William Howe. Most of Longacre's portraits are considered accurate. This portrait is often incorrectly identified as done in 1750. Wooster was not in Quebec until 1754.

Wooster said, "Then it appears their destination is our supply depot in Danbury."

Silliman said, "I deeply regret to inform you, I did not know Danbury was the Crown Forces destination. When they landed at Norwalk they headed east towards my hometown of Fairfield, so I sent a message earlier today to Danbury requesting Colonel Cooke to send me as many soldiers as possible to help repel the invasion. He sent me most of the 1st Connecticut Regiment which were on duty with him."

Silliman realized his decision backfired and left Danbury weakened. He gave a discouraging detail, "I regret to report Colonel Cooke has only about one hundred men with him to defend the depot."

"That is most unfortunate," Wooster said.

Wooster did not criticize Silliman. He put his hand on Silliman's shoulder and said, "You meant well and did the right thing with the information you had."

Wooster was known for his kindness and respect for others. It made him well loved by many.

Arnold saw it was important to reach Danbury. He said, "Then we shall follow General Wooster to Danbury forthwith and stop the Crown Forces!"

Wooster agreed with Arnold's suggestion but said, "General Arnold, I believe that is our best course of action, but the rain has started to come down again and quite intensely, and the wind has picked up making it almost impossible to proceed."

Arnold replied, "I am sure our men are willing to

follow you, through rain and wind."

Wooster said, "I appreciate your confidence in our men, but they are already soaked and tired from marching all day. And making matters worse, two days of rain have made the road extremely muddy and barely passable."

He then said, "Reports say Governor Tryon is leading the invasion and that his invasion force includes men from two regiments which were at Lexington and Concord, and at Bunker Hill. They suffered great loses there. I understand they are looking for revenge."

Arnold added, "It is dangerous to face someone who desires revenge, it makes them fight more passionately."

Silliman agreed with Arnold, "Speaking of revenge, the invasion force also includes a regiment with hundreds of Tories mostly from right here in Fairfield County. They look at us as traitors and would love to see all of us in British prison ships!"

At that time Arnold saw Loyalists as bad, dangerous people. He angrily said, "They are the traitors!"

Wooster said, "You are both correct. The truth is we have only about five hundred men. They have almost two thousand. We are outnumbered about four-to-one."

Wooster showed his understanding of the situation and care for his men. He said, "It would be good for our men to have some rest before we go into battle. I believe we can afford to wait for a reprieve in the rain. That will probably take only an hour or two at most."

He smiled as he said, "You know how quickly the

weather changes here in Connecticut."

Silliman also smiled and said, "That is true. I think it has already changed about four times today."

Wooster replied, "I am sure the weather is just as bad around Danbury and will slow down Tryon and his forces. Hopefully we will arrive before they attack Danbury."

Wooster did not know the Crown Forces were already in Danbury and their intense attack already began.

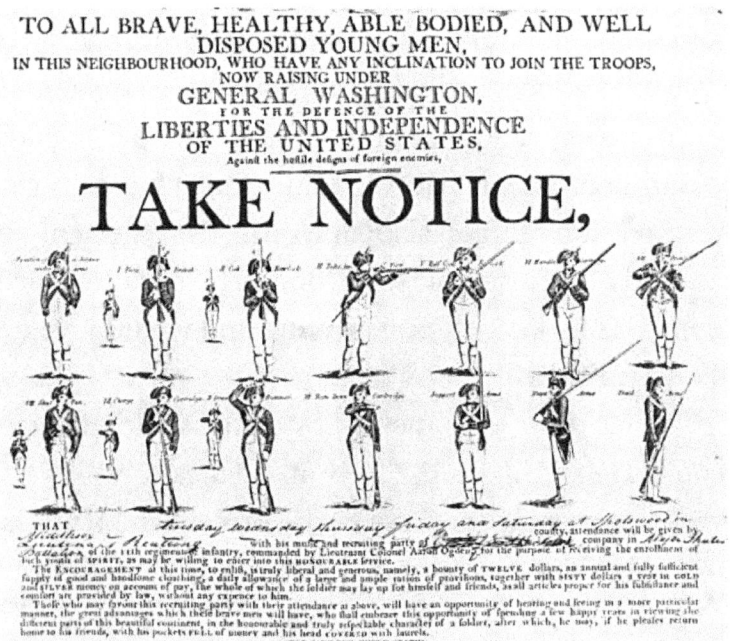

Take Notice Recruitment Poster

This poster is often shown in books as a Revolutionary War recruitment poster. This was not printed until after the war. The officers listed in this poster were members of the 11th Infantry Regiment, which was not formed until 1798.
Printed by B. Jones, Philadelphia, 1798-1815

Chapter 18

Messenger Arrives at Ludington's
April 26, 1777 – Saturday 9 p.m.

It was now Saturday April 26, 1777. It was a cold night in the Hudson Valley. Though some neighboring towns had some relief from the rain it rained steadily in Dutchess County for two days. And it was still raining. The roads were muddy, and the rivers were high.

It was about nine o'clock at night. Colonel Henry Ludington and his wife Abigail were sitting around the fireplace. He was reading and she was mending clothes. Their children were upstairs sleeping except for Sybil and Rebecca. They were still awake talking with each other.

The peaceful silence of the evening was suddenly disturbed by someone pounding on the door.

The Colonel stood up and grabbed his sword. Abigail stopped her work and looked up. She was very concerned, "Henry, who do you think that is?"

Henry replied, "I am not sure."

He looked out the window to see if he could tell who was at the door. It was too dark to see who it was. He could make out was the shape of a man and a horse tied to the post near the door.

With his sword drawn he went to the door and opened it. As he did, the man at the door stumbled into Henry's arms and weakly asked, "Colonel Ludington!"

He was soaking wet and obviously very tired. He did not appear to be a threat. Henry led him to a chair and said, "Abigail, please get a dry blanket for this lad."

Abigail quickly got a blanket. She put it on the messenger. Sybil and Rebecca came downstairs.

Abigail looked at the man shivering. She said, "Let me get you something warm to drink."

She went to the fireplace, got a cup, and filled it from a kettle near the fireplace. She brought it back to him.

Henry said to the messenger, "You are safe now."

The messenger struggled to speak, "Colonel Cooke from Danbury sent me. I rode as fast as I could, but the rain and muddy roads made it difficult."

Sybil and Rebecca stayed back a little. With great concern Sybil asked, "Father, what is happening?"

The messenger said, "The Regulars and Tories attacked and are burning Danbury! It is terrible!"

Abigail was alarmed. She said, "Oh, Henry!"

Alarmed, Sybil and Rebecca each cried, "Father!"

Henry asked the messenger for more information. "When did this happen? How many were there?"

The messenger was holding the mug with both hands. It was his first drink he had since he set out from Danbury, hours ago.

He replied to Henry, "They came after ...." He paused

for a moment trying to gather his thoughts. Then he continued, "After noon, Yes, it was late afternoon."

"I think it was the whole British Army. Colonel Cooke tried to stop them but there were too many!"

Henry asked more questions, "Is Colonel Cooke alright? What about the supplies?"

The messenger took another drink and said, "Last I saw him, Colonel Cooke and a group of our men were still alive. But the Tories and Regulars were taking everything! They were looting and burning piles of things in the street!"

Henry shook his head in concern. He looked at his family and said, "We must call out the Militia!"

He paced around, then said, "We thought they would have attacked the main depot at Fishkill."

Abigail came over to Henry. He put his arms around her. All she could say was, "Oh, Henry!"

This alarming news made Sybil and Rebecca hold tightly to each other.

Henry put his arms out for his daughters. They came over. He put his arms around them and hugged them.

After a few moments he said, "I must stay here and assemble the troops. Abigail, Rebecca, while we wait for the men to arrive I need you to help make as many cartridges for the muskets as we can."

Rebecca replied, "Yes, Father!" Then she and her mother began to get the supplies for making cartridges.

Henry placed his hands on Sybil's shoulders. He looked at her and said, "Sybil, you have been my faithful messenger before. Now I need you to ride again, to call out the Militia, under much more difficult conditions."

As he said that, Abigail stopped what she was doing. She looked at Henry and said, "But Henry! It is raining, and it is so dark! And who knows how many thieves and Tories are waiting to ambush any messenger they see. What about ...?" She was going to suggest the messenger but turned and saw he was sound asleep in the chair.

Henry looked at Abigail. He said, "He is exhausted. There is no other way. It needs to be Sybil."

Abigail was disappointed but knew he was right.

He said, "I know Sybil can do this."

Sybil realized this was very important and did not hesitate. She bravely said, "Oh, Yes, Father! I know the way and I will do my best!"

Sybil was clearly excited at this opportunity. She wanted to do something meaningful for the cause of liberty ever since she heard of the ride of Paul Revere, William Dawes, and Samuel Prescott.

She said, "And I can use my wonderful new horse which Mr. Crosby brought me on my birthday!"

Once Rebecca realized Sybil was going to make the ride she got Sybil's riding boots. She brought them to Sybil and helped her put them on.

Sybil's mother brought her a cloak. She said, "You are going to need this! It is a dreadful rainy night out there."

Abigail then hugged Sybil tightly.

Sybil looked intently at her father.

He said, "You know the route is forty-miles long but

in the dark and rain it will seem like much more than forty miles. Make sure you pace yourself."

Sybil listened closely as her father gave her more instructions, "And as your mother said, you know it is not unusual to find Tories or thieves waiting to ambush anyone who passes by on the road. Perhaps this rain is a good thing, even those type of people usually know enough not to go out on a night like this!"

Abigail grew more concerned, especially when she heard Henry say, *on a night like this*. She ran to Sybil and hugged her again. She said, "Please, be careful!"

Sybil hugged her mother, "Yes, Mother! I will!"

Sybil started to walk towards her Father. Then she looked back at her mother and said, "Please pray for me!"

Her mother replied, "We will Sybil, we will!

Henry spoke as he and Sybil headed to the door, "I know Sybil can do this. This is something God has prepared her for."

Henry and Sybil went outside into the rainy night. They headed to the barn to get her horse ready.

As they were saddling her horse, Henry gave her more instructions, "I am so proud of you Sybil. I know you have always wanted to do your part to help our struggle for liberty. Now the time has come. It is your turn to do what Paul Revere and the others did."

A more serious look came across his face, "But you will be doing so much more. You will be riding alone in the rain and in the dark for a much longer distance."

Sybil replied, "Mehitable Prendergast rode eighty

miles to appeal to the Governor and save her husband. I know I can ride forty miles to save our country!"

She smiled and said, "I will do my best, Father! I know the way! I could almost do it blindfolded!"

Henry said, "I think blindfolded might be a better condition than this rain and darkness. Remember to ride as swiftly as you can! You must be careful. All the snow we had this winter and these spring rains will make some of the streams extra high."

He double-checked her saddle and warned her, "Make sure you avoid as many dark places as you can, it is too dark to see. Do not stop for anyone along the way!"

He then added a word of comfort, "We will pray the rain will stop so you will be able to see better."

He helped Sybil up onto the saddle. He then said, "Sybil, there will not be enough time for you to dismount and knock on each door."

He handed Sybil a stick and said, "Use this stick to wake people up by pounding on the shutters and doors. When they come to their door you will not have time to engage in a conversation. Just tell them, *Call to arms! The Regulars and Tories are burning Danbury! The Militia is needed! Call to arms!*"

He paused and said, "No other explanation is needed they will know what to do. As soon as you deliver that message, go on to the next house, and then on to every other house as fast as you can."

He then gave Sybil one more very important piece of fatherly advice, "And, then, come back home, safe!"

Sybil Rides

Sybil repeated her father's instructions, "Yes, Father! I will say, Call to arms! The Regulars and Tories are burning Danbury! The Militia is needed! Call to arms!"

Henry smiled. He shook his head and said, "Yes, that is right! You have a long hard ride ahead of you!"

Henry looked up toward Heaven. He said a quick prayer, "God, please give Sybil safety as she rides."

Sybil responded with a quick, "Amen!"

Henry gave her horse a swat and said, "God speed!"

Sybil rode off into the rain and began her historic forty-mile ride, to call out the Militia.

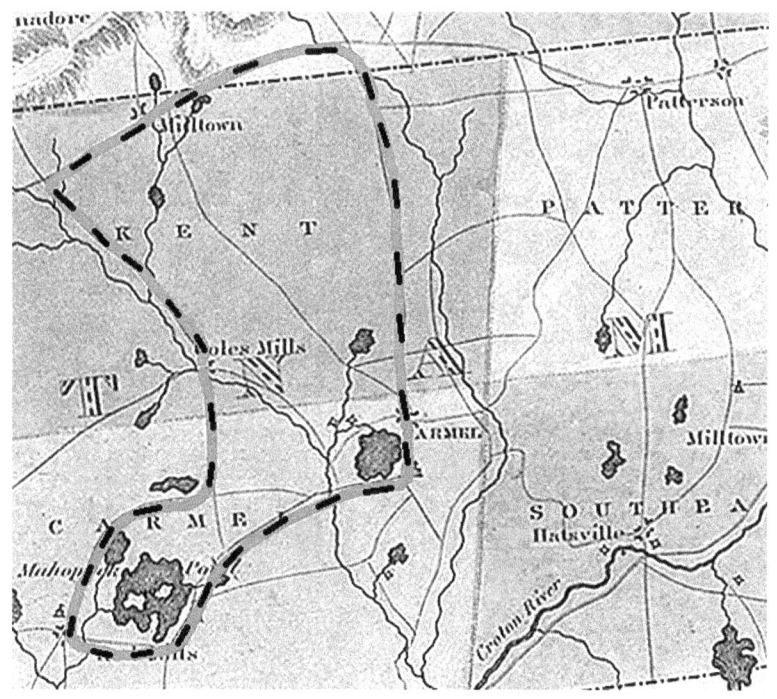

Approximate Route of Sybil's Ride
Approximation on David Burr's 1829 Map.

Chapter 19

Sybil Arrives at the First House
April 26, 1777 – Almost 10 p.m. Saturday

It was almost ten o'clock at night on Saturday, April 26, 1777. Rain had been falling for two days. It was a cold wet night for anyone outside. The roads were wet and muddy. That made it much more difficult to travel.

Sybil left her home a little while ago to call out the Militia. It did not take long for her to get wet and muddy. It also did not take long to reach the first house.

The first house Sybil came to was a simple country home. The lights were off. Everyone inside was asleep.

As Sybil rode up to the front door she pulled back on her horse's reins. She came to a stop. She took the stick her father gave her and banged on the front door of the house. She yelled, "Call to arms! Call to arms!"

She waited a few moments. Then the door to the house opened slowly. A light from a lantern revealed a musket barrel which pointed outside through the door. Sybil did not expect that. She quickly moved back.

It was Samuel, the owner of the house who opened the door. He was asleep when Sybil knocked on the door. Her knocking woke him out of a sound sleep. He quickly jumped out of bed quite alarmed. No one ever came to Samuel's house that late at night. He was concerned because he did not know what to expect. He grabbed his musket, and a lantern, and came to the door.

Simple Colonial Home
Hand Sketch.

He stood there at the door holding the lantern in his left hand. His musket was in his right hand. He was only wearing his night shirt. It hung down to his knees.

Samuel took a step forward. He stuck the lantern a little further out the door. He pointed his musket outside as he spoke gruffly, "Who is it? And what do you want?"

Sybil moved around on her horse and said, "It is I, Sybil Ludington, Colonel Henry Ludington's daughter."

Samuel held the lantern further outside. He wanted a closer look at the rider. The light shone out into the darkness and lit up Sybil. He recognized it truly was her. He then lowered his musket. He said, "Sybil? What are you doing here this late at night and in the rain?!"

Sybil remembered what her father said. She wanted to explain what she was doing but knew there was no time for that. She did as she was told. She gave the message as her father told her, "Call to arms! The Regulars and Tories are burning Danbury! The Militia is needed! Call to arms!"

Samuel was alarmed at the serious message. He replied the way Sybil hoped he would, "Oh No! I will get my son and we will tell the others to come at once!"

Sybil turned and rode off to the next home.

Samuel went back inside. He woke Jedediah his son. They both quickly dressed. They grabbed their muskets and headed to Colonel Ludington's.

Militiaman Prepares to Respond to the Call

*By Benson John Lossing, 1850.
Pictorial Field Book of the Revolution.*

Chapter 20

The Looting and Burning Continue
April 26, 1777 – Very Late Saturday Night

It was very late Saturday night, April 26, 1777. While Sybil was on her ride calling out the Militia the Loyalists continued to loot and burn Danbury. They enjoyed attacking the frightened Rebels. The rain did not slow them down.

Residents of Danbury later reported things became much worse after the soldiers became drunk on the stolen rum.

A family huddled together in fear, inside their home. They tried to avoid the terror taking place around them. They lived close to the main street. They did not have a yard in front of their house. That put them dangerously close to the passing groups of looting Loyalists.

They heard the screaming and gunshots. Those started in the afternoon and continued into the evening. They saw people dragged out of their homes by Loyalists. They Loyalists then took whatever they wanted and then burned down the houses.

They watched the soldiers go up to some homes and then walk away doing no harm. The father noticed there was a ribbon on the door of those homes. He knew some of those houses were the homes of people he suspected had Loyalist leanings. He correctly assumed the ribbons were a signal to protect the Loyalist homes.

The family cowered in a corner in fear for their lives. Shadows of angry men danced across their front windows. Looting Loyalists with torches passed close by their home. They hoped and prayed the looters would pass by and leave their home alone.

They were terrified when three Loyalists walking down the road stopped in front of their house. In the dim light they could see one had a torch in one hand. He had a bottle of rum in the other. The other two men with him were holding muskets. All three were laughing.

The one with the bottle raised it to his mouth. He took a long drink. When he finished drinking, he wiped his mouth and threw it to the ground. He laughed as it smashed in pieces. He then turned toward the house and stared at the window.

As he looked closer at the house the wife gasped. Her husband quickly put his hand over her mouth. They needed to be as quiet as possible, so they would not be detected.

Suddenly they heard a loud boom. It sounded like a musket was fired close by. That made the men in front of the house duck. Then the one who smashed the bottle pointed down the street. He said something to the others.

The men looked down the street where he pointed. Then they raised their muskets and aimed them in the direction he pointed and fired. There was a loud, *Boom!*

The family held each other closer as the musket blast made their front window rattle.

After firing their muskets, the three men moved down the street. The family breathed a great sigh of relief.

Their relief did not last long. Shortly after the three Loyalists left they watched as two more soldiers stopped in front of their window.

Like the first three men, one had a torch in one hand and a bottle in the other. The other had a bottle in one hand and a sack filled with things he stole, slung over his shoulder.

The soldier with the torch in his hand turned towards the house. He held it close to the window moving it back and forth. He was trying to see if anyone was inside. The family tried to hide in fear. They covered their mouths, so they would not scream out in fear.

The soldier thought he saw something inside. He put his face closer to the window. The family thought this would surely be the end for them.

Suddenly they heard another musket blast. The men in front of the window quickly turned. He looked for the source of the musket blast. Then he and the other man quickly moved away.

The family was greatly relieved. The father held them close and said a prayer of thanks.

Chapter 21

Sybil and The Bandits
April 26, 1777 – Very Late Saturday Night

It was cold, rainy, and very late at night on Saturday, April 26, 1777. That was not a good night for traveler's or for bandits. Sybil rode on through the cold and rain.

One of the dangers of travelling around that area, even before the Revolution, was the fact that sometimes there were thieves who waited along the side of the road to rob unsuspecting travelers. Those thieves were usually called *highwaymen*. During the Revolution they became known as either *cowboys* or *skinners*.

Even though it was late at night, and the weather was awful, two desperate bandits waited next to the road that evening. They were hoping some helpless unsuspecting traveler would come their way.

They stood on opposite sides of the road at a place where the road grew narrow. That was the same road Sybil was riding on to call out the Militia. They were waiting for unsuspecting travelers to pass by. They would pounce on them and rob them of anything valuable.

The leader of the two bandits was older than the other. He was wearing a dark heavy wool work shirt. He had an oil cloth draped over his head and shoulders, to help keep him dry. He held a crude wooden club.

He had a not so bright partner who was wearing dark heavy clothing and a wool blanket over his head and shoulders. That blanket was warm but not as effective at keeping off rain as the oil cloth the leader wore. He also carried a wooden club to use on his unsuspecting victims.

Highwaymen Robbing a Traveler

Capture of Major John Andre
By Paulding, Williams & VanWalt.
Lithograph by J. Baillie, 1845

They were outside waiting in the cold and rain for hours. His partner finally complained, "I am so wet and cold! I wish I was someplace with a nice warm fire."

The bandit leader did not like the cold and rain. He was also very uncomfortable, but he believed if they waited long enough their discomfort would be rewarded. He firmly replied to his companion, "Stop your complaining, just think about how rich we are going to be when we catch some unsuspecting traveler."

His partner liked that idea. He shook his head in agreement and said, "I sure would like to be rich!"

The bandit leader said, "Keep thinking about that and be quiet! We do not want anyone to know we are here!"

After a few more minutes of misery his partner asked, "Are you sure someone will be out on a night like this?"

The leader knew it was a bad night to travel but he thought surely someone would have to travel their way. He replied, "Of course they will! This is a main road. People pass by here all the time. And look at it this way, no one will ever suspect we would be out on a night like this and that will make them easy prey."

His partner liked that idea. That made him forget about being wet and cold for a little while.

It was not long after that when the bandit leader heard the sound of someone approaching. He said, "Quiet! I think I hear someone coming! Get ready!"

Both bandits stepped out into the middle of the road. It was dark. They knew no one would see them. They planted their feet firmly and got their clubs ready to attack their unsuspecting prey.

As they stood there waiting for their prize, Sybil came riding up fast in the dark and rain. She did not see them, and they barely saw her.

As she came upon them her horse galloped through a

big murky puddle. A big splash of muddy water flew out of the puddle in all directions, soaking both bandits.

To make matters worse, one of the hooves of Sybil's horse hit the bandit leader in the head. That sent him falling backwards on the cold, wet, muddy ground.

Both bandits were covered with soaking wet mud as Sybil continued to ride on past them. Though they surely noticed her, she never noticed them.

The not so bright partner was shaken up. He wiped some of the mud off his face and said, "What was that?"

The bandit leader shook his head and reluctantly said, "That was the signal for us to go find that warm fire you were talking about."

Chapter 22

Americans Arrive in Bethel
April 26, 1777 – Almost Midnight Saturday

It was almost midnight, Saturday, April 26, 1777. The very tired American Rebel Force led by General David Wooster, General Benedict Arnold, and General Gold Selleck Silliman arrived in Bethel, Connecticut. The Rebel Supply Depot was only a few miles away.

They left Redding about six-thirty in the evening after waiting an hour-and-a-half for a break in the rain. That rest helped refresh the men. The break in the rain allowed them to continue to pursue the Crown Forces.

When they left Redding they soon discovered it was a good thing they had that rest. They did not realize how difficult a struggle the journey was that lay ahead. If it had been daylight they would have seen the road was almost impassable, not just because of two days of rain but because of the deep ruts caused by the Crown Forces and their cannons.

The journey was harder because the sun set before they left Redding. The clouds blocked the light of the moon and stars. Shortly after they left Redding the rain started again. That made it even harder to see and made the journey even more uncomfortable.

When they arrived in Bethel they were all wet, muddy, and very tired. They were frustrated because it took much longer to reach Bethel than they expected.

The thing which discouraged them most was they saw smoke and flames rise from Danbury letting them know the Crown Forces already launched their attack.

Crown Forces Raid and Burn

Reenactors from the Brigade of the American Revolution.
Photograph by Gary Vorwald

General Arnold spoke with some who fled Danbury. They told him how the invaders went beyond taking the supplies and started looting and setting on fire the homes of those not loyal to the Crown. They saw people dragged from their homes and others killed.

General Arnold found General Wooster and gave his report. He said, "General Wooster, as you know, the Crown Forces attacked Danbury. I learned Colonel Cooke put up a valiant defense, but the opposing force was too great. And, the Crown Forces not only stole our supplies but got into a drunken rage and burned homes and murdered people!"

Silliman also spoke with refuges. He confirmed what Arnold said. "Yes, General Arnold, people told me the same things and said, the Tories were the worst of the lot!" He paused, then angrily said, "If I had my way all traitors would be hung!"

Arnold and Wooster shook their heads in agreement. They both firmly said, "Yes!"

Arnold was very angry, he said, "We need to go and stop them!"

Wooster was shaken by the news. He said, "I would like to do that, but our men are exhausted, and our powder is wet. You know wet powder renders our muskets useless. We would not stand a chance against them without our muskets."

Silliman wanted to attack but saw wisdom in Wooster's words, "No matter how much I would like to stop this atrocity, I believe we have to wait until morning to attack."

Arnold wanted to attack but agreed it was best to wait for the morning. He firmly said, "In the morning when they are hung over and confident we will strike them hard and if we cannot defeat them we will drive them back into the sea."

Wooster was pleased with their response and said, "We will show them our resolve and our love for liberty!"

"For liberty!" echoed Arnold and Silliman.

Chapter 23

Sybil Arrives at Another Home
April 27, 1777 – Long Before Sunrise Sunday

It was Sunday, April 27, 1777, long before sunrise. The rain was still falling but not as hard. The Crown Forces were still looting and burning Danbury. The Rebels were resting in Bethel. They planned to attack in the morning. Sybil was still riding.

She was soaking wet from riding in the rain and along muddy roads for many hours. She was terribly tired but faithfully pressed on.

Sybil stopped at many houses giving the call to arms. At each stop men responded. They headed to Colonel Ludington's. Some went on horseback. Some went in wagons and others on foot.

She rode up to another house. She pounded on the door with her stick as she did at the other houses.

She yelled, "Call to arms!" and waited for a response.

When no one responded she pounded again and yelled, "Call to arms!"

Finally, a man slowly opened the door. He was shaken out of a nice deep sleep by Sybil's call and pounding. He was barely awake as he jumped out of bed. He grabbed a lantern and headed to the door.

As he opened the door he poked the lantern outside and held the door with his other hand. Sybil noticed he looked like he had been sleeping very hard.

He was surprised when the lantern revealed a soaking wet girl on a horse with a stick in her hands. He thought he recognized her. He was not quite sure if he was awake or dreaming.

Sybil looked at him and said, "Call to arms! The Regulars and Tories are burning Danbury! The Militia is needed! Call to arms!"

The man just stood there. This was not at all what he expected to find at his door in the middle of the night.

As soon as Sybil finished giving her call she turned and rapidly rode off to the next house.

The man stood in the doorway of his house for a few moments. He was in a daze. He wondered if he was dreaming.

He thought he recognized the girl on the horse as Sybil Ludington, Colonel Henry Ludington's daughter. He wondered why he was dreaming Sybil would come to his house in the middle of the night.

He stood there for a few more moments, thinking about what just happened. Suddenly he realized this was not a dream, he was indeed awake. Sybil's message finally sunk in. He was in the Militia and realized he needed to respond to the call right away.

He left the door open as he quickly headed back into his house to get the rest of his clothes on. He grabbed his musket and headed out the door to go to Colonel Ludington's. He did not think about the danger only that he was needed to respond to help defend freedom.

Colonial Militia Respond to the Call

By Felix Octavius Car Darley, 1877.

Chapter 24

Making Ammunition

April 27, 1777 – Sunday Long Before Sunrise

It was the wee hours of the morning on Sunday, April 26, 1777. If it had been a normal night, everyone in Colonel Henry Ludington's family would have been asleep for many hours. This was not a normal night.

A British force of close to two thousand men were looting and burning Danbury, Connecticut. A messenger from Colonel Joseph Platt Cooke, arrived hours ago asking for help. Colonel Ludington's oldest daughter, sixteen-year old Sybil Ludington was riding through the dark rainy night to call out the Militia.

Sybil's family were all awake helping prepare for the Militia to arrive. Colonel Ludington's wife Abigail, their daughter Rebecca, and son Archibald were making cartridges. That is the ammunition used in muskets. Mary and Henry, Jr., were helping by playing with their younger brother Tertullus and watching their baby sister.

To make cartridges for the muskets one person cut out pieces of old newspaper to the proper size.

The next person used a wood dowel, with a musket ball at the end, and rolled the paper around the dowel and ball. Then they twisted the end near the ball closed. Sometimes they tied a piece of string around the outside above the musket ball, but they did not do that this time.

The next person poured black powder into each cartridge. Then they folded the last end closed.

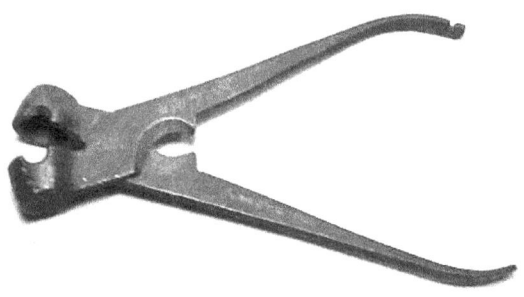

18th Century Musket Ball Mold & Tool

Musket Ball trimmer between handles.

Making the musket balls was Colonel Ludington's job. He melted lead in a small cast iron pot over coals at the edge of the fireplace. He then poured the melted lead into a mold. That formed a small round musket ball. He then trimmed off the edge which was left on the musket ball by the mold. Then he put the completed ones in a small bowl on the table.

When the Militia arrived later they would grab handfuls of the ammunition and fill their cartridge pouches. Most pouches held nineteen rounds in a wood block. Additional cartridges were placed under the block.

Rebecca was glad she could help while her sister Sybil was calling out the Militia.

Rebecca said, "Father, I am glad we can help make these cartridges for the soldiers."

Henry smiled. He then spoke, showing the importance of what they were doing, "Your help is greatly appreciated. Every man will come with some cartridges, but we need to make as many as we can."

He then said, "I fear we will be engaged in a fierce battle and we will need many more cartridges than the men will have with them."

Abigail looked up from her task. She spoke with motherly concern, "I pray Sybil is alright!"

Henry spoke to reassure her, "I am sure the Lord is watching out for her."

Suddenly their conversation was interrupted by someone banging on their front door. The family stopped what they were doing. They looked at each other with a look of concern on their faces.

Henry picked up his sword. He headed to the door. He carefully opened the door with his sword drawn.

There were two soaking wet people standing at the door. It was Samuel, the man from the first home which Sybil came to. His son Jedediah was with him.

They held muskets in their hands. Water dripped off their hats and off the wet wool blankets draped over their shoulders. They were soaked from making their way through the pouring rain to the Ludington's.

When they saw Colonel Ludington standing there with his sword in his hand, they took a step back.

Samuel quickly said, "No need for that Colonel! It is

me Samuel and my son Jedediah!"

Henry smiled. He lowered his sword and invited them in, "Samuel, Jedediah! Come inside out of the rain!"

Samuel and Jedediah entered the house. They were so wet, water continued to drip off them.

Samuel said, "We got the message from Sybil that the Regulars and Tories are burning Danbury. We are here to help drive them back to the sea."

Inside a Typical Colonial Home
*Very typical image of items found in a colonial home.
Cooking was done in the fireplace.
H.W. Pearce, 1876 Engraving.*

His son, Jedediah got an angry look on his face and said, "I would like to drive them all the way back across the ocean to their King George!"

Henry replied, "That sounds like a good idea."

Abigail Ludington poured some coffee for them. Before handing them the cups she said, "Take off those wet things and have a cup of coffee to warm you up."

They took off their hats and wool blankets and gladly received the warm cups from Abigail.

As they started to drink their coffee there was another knock at the door.

This time when Colonel Ludington opened the door three men stood there. It was a father and his two teenage sons. Just like Samuel and Jedediah all three were carrying muskets and were soaking wet.

Colonel Ludington knew they were in his Militia. He smiled as he said, "Come in!"

The younger of the two sons walked over to where the Colonel's family were making cartridges.

He looked at Rebecca and smiled. He was very pleased to see her. She smiled back at him. She seemed very pleased to see him too.

He asked, "Can we help?"

Rebecca moved over to make room and said, "Oh yes! We can use all the help we can get."

The younger son smiled. He signaled his brother to come over to the table and help make cartridges.

There was another knock on the door.

Colonel Ludington headed to answer the door.

Men Militia continued to arrive. They all responded to Sybil's call and came to fight for liberty and to help drive the Crown Forces back into the sea.

Chapter 25

Sybil Faces an Obstacle
April 27, 1777 – Sunday Long Before Sunrise

It was a long time before the sun would rise on Sunday, April 27, 1777. It was a welcomed relief when the rain finally stopped in that part of Dutchess County. But the roads were wet and muddy from two days of steady rain. That made them much harder to travel on. The two days of rain also caused the rivers and streams to overflow. That made them very difficult to pass in many places. This was a bad time for someone to be traveling.

One person travelling at that difficult time was Sybil Ludington. She was riding to call out the men in her Father's Militia. The roads she travelled on passed through many streams. Many of those streams were high and were overflowing their banks.

Sybil came galloping down the road and approached one of the overflowing streams. Throughout the night she jumped over some other brooks on her horse. This one presented a more serious obstacle. This stream was overflowing to the point where its banks were completely covered with raging water. It looked like there was no way to safely cross that stream.

Sybil rode up along the stream looking for a safe way to cross. It might have been possible to find a safe place to cross if it were not so dark out. She turned her horse around and rode in the other direction. To complete her mission, she had to cross that stream. She was upset because she unable to find a safe place to cross.

She rode back to the road where she first faced the obstacle of this swollen stream. This was a very difficult discouraging situation. Though she could not find a safe place to cross she decided she was not going to allow that to stop her. She was determined to complete her mission.

Sybil spoke to her horse, "There is no easy way around this one Star, but we have to cross this stream."

She looked up toward Heaven and said a quick prayer, "Lord, I need your help on this one!"

With a disregard for the danger, Sybil urged her horse forward. They headed boldly into the dangerously overflowing stream.

The rapidly rushing water pressed hard and strong against them. It made it very difficult to go forward, but they continued to press on. It was an extremely hard struggle to find sure footing. Still, Sybil and her horse, continued to slowly move forward.

Suddenly her horse lost his footing. He started to slip. Sybil was afraid he would fall and break a leg. That would end their ride and maybe his life. She was very thankful when he quickly regained his footing. They continued to press on. They finally came out safe on the other side.

Once they were safely across the stream, Sybil looked back for a moment. Then she looked up and said, "Thank you!"

She then tightened up on the reins and rode on with her mission.

She would face more streams on her ride but that was the most difficult one. She was very thankful she faced that obstacle and overcame it.

Overflowing Stream in Putnam County
This is one of the swollen streams Sybil crossed on her forty-mile ride, to call out the Militia.
Photograph by Larry A. Maxwell, Spring 2018

Chapter 26

Militia March off to Battle
April 27, 1777 – Before Sunrise Sunday Morning

It was about an hour before sunrise on Sunday, April 27, 1777. Sybil Ludington was still riding throughout lower Dutchess County calling out the Militia. She gave the call to arms at each house. The men then left their homes and headed to the Militia Training Ground next to Colonel Henry Ludington's home in Fredericksburg.

All through the night the Militia arrived. By about an hour before sunrise there were about two hundred men, standing in small groups in the field across from the Colonel's home. Colonel Ludington, Lieutenant Colonel Reuben Ferris and Captain Edmund Baker stood together talking.

Jabez and Judah Chase came up to Colonel Ludington. Jabez said, "Colonel, we got the message from Sybil and came right away."

His brother Judah let him to know they, and the other men, were coming because of Sybil, "The whole countryside is responding thanks to your daughter."

Henry replied with a big smile.

When Colonel Ludington saw many of his men arrived, he turned to Ferris and Baker. He said, "It is time to call the men together."

Captain Baker yelled, "Fall in!" That was the command to call the troops together.

The men lined up in two rows. Their muskets rested on their left shoulders.

Baker then yelled the next order, "Order, arms!"

Each man put the butt of his musket near his right foot. Their right hand then held their musket near the end of the barrel as they put their left arm by their side.

Colonel Ludington came forward to speak to the troops. Captain Baker was on one side and Lieutenant Colonel Ferris on his other side.

The Colonel gave the command, "Take your ease."

Captain Baker echoed, "Take your ease!"

The men took a more relaxed position.

Colonel Ludington began to speak to them with respect, urgency, and passion, "All of you heard the alarm sounded by my daughter Sybil."

One of the men shouted, "Three Huzzahs for Sybil!"

In response to his call all the men grabbed their hats with their left hand. They waved them in the air as they shouted, "Huzzah! Huzzah! Huzzah!"

Colonel Ludington was obviously pleased by the men's cheer for his daughter. After they were done he nodded his head in thanks. Then he continued speaking, "I want to thank every one of you for responding to the call. I know these are not the ideal circumstances to be given a call, but you still came, and I am deeply grateful."

The Colonel gave more details of why they were called, "As most of you know by now, the British Regulars and a large Tory Regiment have attacked our supply depot at Danbury. They stole our supplies of food, clothing, guns, and power. Those supplies were important to help our struggle for independence."

He paused as a more serious look came across his face. He then continued, "They set many building on fire and have taken prisoners!"

One of the men yelled out with great concern, "I have family in Danbury!"

A few others spoke up saying, "Me too!"

Colonel Ludington replied, "I know many of you have family and friends in Danbury and I know you are concerned for their safety."

He then gave an important update, "I received word from another messenger, that General Wooster, General Silliman and General Benedict Arnold are at Bethel and plan to attack the Crown Forces in Danbury in the morning. They plan to drive them back to the sea and want our help!"

He paused, then asked, "Are you with me?!"

All the men took off their hats. They waved them in the air and yelled, "Huzzah! Huzzah! Huzzah!"

As Colonel Ludington was talking more men arrived.

After the cheer from his men the Colonel continued to speak. "I will take those of you who are here now, and we will head to Danbury."

He looked at Lieutenant Colonel Ferris and said, "Lieutenant Colonel Ferris will stay here and wait for the rest of the men and will follow us forthwith."

Ferris nodded his head and said, "Yes, Colonel!"

Colonel Ludington looked at the troops again and yelled, "Are you ready to do your part for liberty lads?!"

The men again took off their hats. They waved them in the air and shouted, "Huzzah! Huzzah! Huzzah!"

Revolutionary War Militiaman on Horse

This painting is called Israel Putnam Leaving His Plow. Most Militia were notified by a messenger on horseback.
Yale University Art Gallery, New Haven, CT.

The Continental Army and militia from larger towns normally marched from place to place by foot. The men in Colonel Ludington's militia lived in a very rural area. Most of them lived quite a distance from one another. They responded on horseback or came in a horse-drawn wagon by themselves. Some picked up their neighbors on the way. Very few responded on foot.

The Colonel spoke, "For us to arrive in time to be of any help we need to have every man on a horse or in a wagon. If any of you responded to the call on foot I want you to ride with those who came with their wagons. Those of you who came with your wagons take as many men, who came by foot, with you in your wagons. If there is not enough room in the wagons then some of you may need to take another man with you on your horse."

He paused then gave the command, "You are dismissed to form up on your horses and in the wagons!"

Captain Baker echoed the command, "Dismissed to form up on your horses and in the wagons!"

Colonel Ludington had one group on horseback in the front with him. One group rode with the wagons. Another group ride in the back as a rear guard.

He watched to make sure all the men were on horseback or in a wagon. He then rode to the font of the line. He then yelled, "Forward to Danbury! We shall drive the enemy back to the sea!"

All the men shouted another round of "Huzzah!"

They rode off determined to make a difference.

Lieutenant Colonel Ferris stayed behind waiting for the rest of the men to arrive.

Chapter 27

Sybil at the Ganong's
April 27, 1777 – Before Sunrise Sunday Morning

It was before sunrise on Sunday, April 27, 1777. The Crown Forces were still looting and burning Danbury. Sybil Ludington was riding all night to call out the Militia. She now came to another home. When she realized, it was the Ganong's home she almost did not stop.

Sybil Rides on Through the Night

Ericka Rose portrays Sybil at Sybil Rides 240th Event
Living History Guild Photograph

Her friend, Jesse Ganong, lived there. He wanted to join the Militia but his father, John Ganong, would not allow him to join. His father was a successful businessman. He had dealings with people with Loyalist leanings. He believed the Revolution was a bad misunderstanding. He thought it would end soon if people stopped making the Crown angry. He thought it was safe to stay as neutral as possible.

Sybil decided she should ride up to the house and give the call. She rode up and banged on the front door with her stick, just as she did at all the other houses. She then yelled, "Call to arms! Call to arms!"

In a few moments, the front door opened slightly. Jesse's father, John Ganong, was standing there in his nightshirt holding a small lantern.

John tried to see who would be calling at this time of night. As he looked out the door he saw a soaking wet person on a horse. He thought it looked like Sybil Ludington. He was confused, why would Sybil be at their home at such a strange hour?

He called to the rider, "Sybil? Is that you?"

Sybil responded, "Yes, Sir!"

John asked, "What are you doing here?!"

She knew John Ganong was against his son Jesse being in the Militia but decided she must give the call.

She said, "Call to arms! The Regulars and Tories are burning Danbury! The Militia is needed! Call to arms!"

That news was not something John was expecting. He was hoping things would get better. He did not expect there would be an attack especially one as close as Danbury. He never thought something like this would happen. He was greatly alarmed.

He stepped back a little. He said, "This cannot be! They would not attack Danbury!"

Jesse came to the door. He pushed past his father. He came out of the house putting on his frock coat and hat.

Jesse looked at Sybil. He said, "Sybil, I heard your call! I do not have a musket, but I want to help!"

Sybil smiled. She was very glad to hear that. She replied, "Father will give you one."

She turned and rode off, on to the next house.

Jesse got his horse ready. He then started to head in the direction from which Sybil rode up to the house.

His father stood there in disbelief. He was hoping it was a bad dream, but knew it really was happening as he saw Jesse riding off.

He yelled to his son, "Jesse! Do not go!"

Jesse yelled back to his Father, "Father, I must go!"

The last thing his father heard Jesse say, as he rode off into the night was, "I must fight for liberty!".

John Ganong stood in the door of his house for a moment shaking his head in disbelief. He said, "This is terrible!"

John put his head in his hands and slowly walked back into the house. He was concerned about his future, he said, "Oh no! What are we going to do?"

Chapter 28

Crown Forces Leave Danbury
April 27, 1777 – Early Sunday Morning

It was early in the morning on Sunday, April 27, 1777. The town of Danbury was burning as the Crown Forces started to leave the city. Some soldiers were leading groups of prisoners taken during the raid. Stolen wagons were loaded with Rebel supplies. Some Loyalists pushed or pulled two-wheeled carts overflowing with goods they took from Rebel homes. Others carried what they took in sacks slung over their shoulders.

Governor William Tryon, General James Agnew, General William Erskine, and General Montfort Browne were standing together at the edge of town. They were in in a very happy mood talking about their victory, everyone except Erskine.

Browne spoke full of price, "That will teach the Rebel scum what happens when they are disloyal to their king!"

Tryon responded with some sarcasm, "General Browne, I see your men enjoyed the rum they found!"

Browne smiled with a smug look on his face, "They do deserve to celebrate a job well done!"

Crown Forces Leaving Town
Photograph by Gary Vorwald

Erskine was very upset. He was a career military man who believed strongly in military protocol. Looting and burning the homes of civilians was not acceptable to him. He had to say something. He spoke out showing he was not happy, "That was not proper military protocol!"

His comment surprised the group. Tryon agreed with Erskine but was glad the raid was a success. He sought to soften a tense moment, "You are right General Erskine, but I cannot argue with success."

Erskine liked a military victory, but believed this military victory was ruined by the improper actions of Browne's Loyalists. He felt he must show he was not pleased or further "successes" could be ruined by such unacceptable actions.

He spoke out again, "I am not sure I call it a success

when our soldiers are supposed to gather supplies and burn what we cannot carry away, yet instead they get drunk and burn down a city!"

Browne acted like he was not affected at all by Erskine's comments. He was enjoying his success and the support he thought he had from Tryon. He would not accept Erskine's scolding because he had no problem with the actions of his men.

Browne replied to Erskine's, "They should burn every Rebel home and hang them all by the neck!"

Erskine felt disgust for Browne and responded with a warning, "I am sure this is going to cause them to retaliate against us with extreme vengeance."

Browne laughed and said, "While they run away from us!"

Tryon felt it best to ignore the conversation between Erskine and Browne. He changed the subject by signaling one of his junior officers, who was holding a map, to come close. Tryon had him hold one end of the map while he called another aide over to hold the other end open.

Tryon then pointed to the map and spoke, "They will expect us to go back the same way we came."

He pointed to the map and said, "Look here."

The others looked where Tryon pointed on the map. Erskine still had an angry look on his face.

As he pointed at the map, Tryon said, "We will go back along a different route, here through Ridgefield."

Erskine liked that idea. He was glad he was finally able to express his approval of something. "Excellent plan Governor!"

Tryon closed the map and said, "We will be back safe in our ships and on our way back to New York before the Rebels know what hit them!"

Erskine expressed his concern, "I hope you are right!"

Browne proudly responded, "Trust me, the Rebels have run away and are hiding from us. We have seen all the resistance we are going to see!"

Erskine looked at Brown with an angry look.

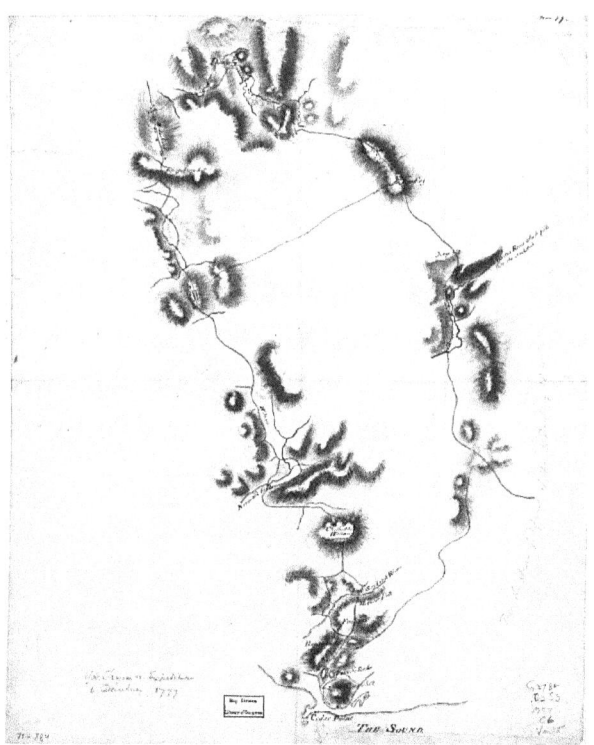

1777 Map of Tryon's Raid on Danbury

By John Montresor
Montressor was the Chief British Engineer in North America.
The Library of Congress, Washington, D.C.

 **Chapter 29**

Sybil Rides as the Sun Rises
April 27, 1777 – Sunrise Sunday

It was the morning of Sunday, April 27, 1777. After a cold rainy night, the sun finally rose and peaked over the hills in Dutchess County, New York.

The Crown Forces finished their raid on Danbury and were on their way back to their ships in Norwalk. They took a different route heading through Ridgefield. They were encouraged they only faced some unorganized resistance from small groups of Militia along the way.

They did not know, all night long Militia in lower Dutchess County New York, responded to the call from sixteen-year old Sybil Ludington. They began to assemble on the training ground across from the home of Colonel Henry Ludington. The first group of two hundred men left with the Colonel a few hours ago. Lieutenant Colonel Reuben Ferris waited behind for the rest of the men to arrive before he would leave with them.

Sybil rode all night long on cold wet muddy roads. She went from house to house, calling out the Militia through the cold, dark and rain. She faced obstacles along the way but kept going on.

When the rain stopped in Dutchess County a few hours ago, that was a real blessing. But the rest of the night was still cold and dark, and Sybil was very wet. Her cold wet clothing was draining her strength. She was extremely tired but there was no time to rest. There were still many more homes she had to reach with the call to arms. There were still many miles she had to ride before her task would be complete.

Sunrise Over the Hills
Engraving by Andrews from Wheelock drawing, 1860.

As the sun started to rise, its rays not only drove away the darkness but also began to spread their warmth. That warmth not only spread over the wet chilly earth but also began to warm anyone outside under its rays.

As the sun broke through the trees and shone upon Sybil, it started to warm her wet rain-soaked clothing.

The warmth slowly spread from her clothing to her body. The higher the sun rose the brighter it became.

The sun's rays became warmer and warmer. They started to dry Sybil's wet clothing and warmed her spirit. That was a welcome relief which brought a smile to her face.

When Sybil came to a clearing where the sun was shining bright, she stopped for a moment. She spread her arms wide and soaked in the warm rays of the sun.

She then looked up and said, "Thank you!"

Sybil was still very tired and not completely dry, but those few moments in the sun gave her an added spark of energy.

She put her head back down. She tightened up her horse's reins and rode on to call out the rest of the Militia.

Chapter 30

American Officers Plan Response
April 27, 1777 – Early Sunday Morning

It was early in the morning on Sunday, April 27, 1777. A light rain continued on and off throughout the night but finally stopped. The Crown Forces, which raided Danbury throughout the night, left not long after sunrise. They were heading back to their ships by a different route, one that would take them through Ridgefield, Connecticut.

Sunrise saw the American Rebel Force under General David Wooster, General Benedict Arnold, and General Gold Selleck Silliman prepare to depart from Bethel and head to Danbury. They planned to launch an attack and drive away the invaders.

Right before they set out, scouts whom General Wooster sent out earlier, reported back that the Crown Forces left Danbury and were on their way to Ridgefield.

Wooster called Arnold and Silliman together to update them. When they reached him, he was looking at a map of the area with his aides.

Wooster pointed at the map. He said, "General Arnold, General Silliman, I was looking at this map which shows the area between Danbury and Norwalk."

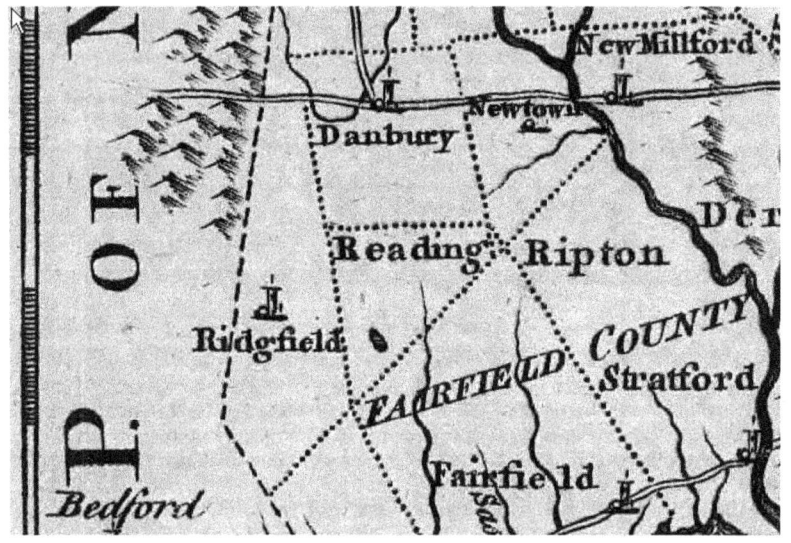

Colonial Fairfield County Connecticut
Map by Thomas Kitchen, 1758.

He told them, "Our scouts reported Tryon and his men have left Danbury and are heading back along a different route than the way they came. They are heading back to Norwalk by way of Ridgefield."

General Arnold looked with interest at the map and the possible route of the Crown Forces. Earlier that day he wrote a letter to Brigadier General Alexander McDougall stating he thought the Crown Forces were marching on to Fishkill and then Peekskill. He did not expect them to go back to Norwalk.

Arnold was wondering what to do when Wooster

looked at each of the generals and said, "Gentlemen now it is our time to show them how we respond to injustice!"

Arnold and Silliman agreed with what Wooster said. They nodded in agreement.

Arnold said, "We must show them our resolve!"

Wooster said, "It is important to show the Crown Forces we will not just sit by and let them get away with such horrendous actions. I know we are greatly outnumbered but we must respond as the Militia did two years ago in response to the attack on Lexington and Concord."

He said, "Remember how those brave, dedicated men inflicted significant damage to the retreating British Regulars. I hope we too can inflict such damage to the retreating Regulars and their Tory allies."

He pointed at the map as he said, "General Silliman, General Arnold, I need the two of you to take four hundred men and proceed to Ridgefield, to cut them off."

He looked up and said, "I sent messengers to have Colonel Bradley and the 5th Connecticut Regiment go to Ridgefield. I also sent messengers to the Yorkers under Colonel Drake and Colonel Ludington to join you there."

Arnold and Silliman nodded in agreement.

Wooster continued, "I will take the remaining men, along with Colonel Jedediah Huntington and the 1st Connecticut Regiment, and we will launch a rear attack."

Arnold agreed, "Excellent plan General Wooster! We will have them trapped!"

Wooster appreciated the compliment but said, "We

may not be able to stop them, but we will make them pay!"

The others agreed.

Wooster then said his last words, "With God's help we will indeed show them our resolve!"

Colonel Jedediah Huntington
*He commanded the 1st Connecticut Regiment.
Engraving by A.H. Richie from a painting by Col. Trumbull.*

Chapter 31

Opposition South of Danbury
April 27, 1777 – About 9 a.m. Sunday

It was Sunday morning April 27, 1777. Shortly after sunrise the rain stopped. The Crown Forces were marching down the road heading from Danbury towards Ridgefield, back to their fleet at Compo Beach.

The soldiers were tired from a long day and night but were in good spirits, especially since the rain stopped.

Two Loyalist friends talked with each other as they headed down the road. Each had a musket in one hand and a sack slung over one shoulder. The sacks were filled with things they took from Rebel homes.

The older looking one smiled as he said to the younger, "I am so glad it stopped raining."

His friend smiled and agreed, "So am I."

The older looking one spoke about their raid. He had a smile on his face as he said, "That was fun!"

His friend smiled and said, "Yes it was! "The Rebel scum never knew what hit them!"

Some Rebel Militia moved through the woods quietly toward the Crown Forces. They came undetected, close to the road, near the two Loyalist friends.

The Militia officer commanded his men, "Spread out along the wall and behind the trees, quietly!"

The Crown Forces continued marching along cheerfully, with a false sense of security. A Militiaman pointed his musket at one of the Loyalists. He slowly but firmly pulled the trigger. Two others did the same. As the muskets fired they made a very loud, *Boom!*

Militiamen Attack Crown Forces

Militia shoot then quickly disappear.
Living History Guild Achieve Photo.

The older looking Loyalist, and a man behind him, were each hit by a musket ball. As they fell to the ground fear gripped the hearts of the others.

A Loyalist officer ran to the edge of the road to take control. He quickly called his men to action. He yelled the command, "Form a line!"

The friend of the older Loyalist dropped his sack. He quickly put his musket on his left shoulder and formed a line with the other Loyalists facing the woods. They stood in fear as they saw smoke from the muskets in the woods.

The Loyalist officer yelled, "Prime and load!"

As soon as he gave that command, and while his men started to follow his command, another Rebel fired his musket. The bullet from that musket hit the officer. He grabbed his chest and fell to the ground.

The soldiers standing near him were filled with fear as they watched him drop. They looked at the woods as they loaded their muskets. More musket shots were heard. Another soldier was hit and fell backwards.

A second Loyalist officer quickly came forward and took the first officer's place. He yelled out the orders, "Make Ready! Present! Fire!"

The Loyalists fired their muskets. Smoke filled the air. The Militia quickly and quietly moved away.

Loyalists Return Fire

Reenactors from the Brigade of the American Revolution.
Photograph by Gary Vorwald, 2014

Chapter 32

Sybil at the Last Home
April 27, 1777 – 9 a.m. Sunday

It was Sunday morning, April 27, 1777. The sun rose a few hours earlier and helped dry off Sybil Ludington's wet clothing. She was exhausted from riding all night. By this time, she rode almost forty miles on a loop calling out the Militia. Her task was almost complete.

An older couple was seated inside their small country home that Sunday morning. They were eating a simple breakfast, before going to church.

Their meal was interrupted by a pounding sound on their door. They rose from their seats and went to the door to see who was there. When the man opened the door, he saw Sybil Ludington. She was slumped down on her horse.

Sybil looked up and tried to shout. Her voice was almost gone. With a weak voice she said, "Call to arms! The Regulars and Tories are burning Danbury! The Militia is needed! Call to arms!"

The woman thought she recognized Sybil. She asked, "Sybil Ludington? Is that you?"

Kitchen in a Typical Colonial Home
*The fireplace was the center of the home.
1940"s postcard of a colonial home.*

Sybil replied wearily, "Yes, Ma'am."

The woman was concerned when she saw how tired Sybil looked. She wanted to help her. She said, "Oh, my dear! You look exhausted! Please come inside and warm yourself up by the fire and have something to eat!"

Normally, Sybil would have accepted that invitation. She responded politely but said, "Thank you very much, but there is no time for that."

The woman realized Sybil must have been riding for a long time. She asked, "How long have you been riding?"

Sybil was very tried. She knew she had to leave and head towards home, but responded politely, "Since about nine o'clock last night, Ma'am."

When the woman first saw Sybil, she thought maybe

Sybil rose early in the morning, then rode to their home. She was surprised to learn how long Sybil was riding.

She said. "My dear it is nine o'clock in the morning. You have been riding all night!"

As Sybil turned to ride away she said, "God gives me the strength I need! I must go on!"

The woman said, "We will be praying for you!"

The man grabbed his musket. He kissed wife and headed out the door and on to Colonel Ludington's to join the rest of the Militia to go fight for liberty.

Historical Marker for Sybil's Ride
One of the numerous historical markers placed by the New York State Department of Education in 1935, to identify the route of Sybil's ride. This one is on Route 52, next to Lake Gleneida (previously Shaw's Pond).
Photograph by Larry A. Maxwell, 2017

Chapter 33

Wooster Attacks the Crown Forces
April 27, 1777 – Late Sunday Morning

It was late morning on Sunday, April 27, 1777. The Crown Forces were marching down the road towards Ridgefield for a few hours. They encountered only a little resistance on the way. That was about to change.

An artillery crew, toward the rear of the Crown Forces, heard some occasional musket fire along the way but had not been fired upon. They were thankful for that.

What they heard was the sound of General David Wooster with the 1st Connecticut Regiment, attacking the very far end of the Crown Forces' line.

It was not long before they saw General William Erskine rapidly riding on his horse toward them. He was waving his sword over his head.

Erskine yelled, "The Rebels are behind us lads!"

Those words sent shivers down their spines.

Erskine yelled, "Get that gun turned around and show them what happens when they oppose the King's Army!"

The artillery crew stopped. They turned their cannon around and struggled to move their cannon to the rear to face the enemy. The muddy road made that difficult, but they finally managed to get in position.

One of the British officers yelled, "Load the cannon."

He then yelled, "Infantry form a line on each side of the cannon!"

The Regulars formed two rows on each side of the cannon with their muskets.

The cannon crew loaded their cannon. They ran the worm down the barrel, then the sponge. A charge was then put in the barrel and rammed in place. One of the artillery men inserted a pick into the touchhole, preparing for a metal tube, loaded with powder which served as the fuse. Now the cannon was ready to fire.

While the cannon crew were loading, the officer ordered the infantry to do load their muskets. He yelled, "Prime and load!"

When the soldiers finished loading, they came to the *Ready* position. Now both the cannon and the infantry were loaded and ready to fire.

The officer then yelled another command to the infantry, "Front row, take a knee."

In one swift movement the front row of soldiers went down on one knee with their muskets pointed ahead. They waited for the Rebels to appear.

For the past few hours Major General David Wooster, along with men from the 1st Connecticut Regiment of the Continental Army and some local Militiamen, marched hard and fast towards Ridgefield. They first made a small attack. Now they came back to strike another blow. This time there was a cannon facing them.

As the Crown Forces saw Wooster and his men draw close, one of their officers yelled, "Fire!"

The cannon and infantry fired at the same time.

A cannon ball plowed across the field and musket balls flew past Wooster and his men.

Wooster yelled, "Come on my boys, never mind such random shots!"

He then yelled to his men, "Halt!"

His men quickly came to a halt.

Wooster gave orders which his men immediately followed. They were already loaded so he gave the firing commands, "Make Ready! Present! Fire!"

Wooster's troops pointed their muskets at their enemy. They all fired at the same time.

He then quickly yelled to his men, "Fire at will!"

Wooster's troops reloaded. Then each man started to shoot as fast as he could at the Crown Forces.

The Crown Forces returned another round of fire. A thundering boom shook the ground. Smoke clouded the view and made it hard to see.

When the smoke started to clear a little it revealed Wooster was hit and knocked off his horse.

One of Wooster's men rushed to help him.

He yelled, "General Wooster! You have been hit!" He stayed close by his side.

The Crown Forces reloaded and fired again.

As soon as they fired the officer yelled another set of commands, "Front Row! Stand! Prime and Load!"

The soldiers stood, loaded their muskets and were ready to fire again.

Wooster's troops returned fire. A few soldiers fell.

The British officer then yelled , "Fix, bayonets!"

The sound of them fixing their bayonets filled the air.

The officer then extended his sword towards the Rebels and yelled, "Charge!"

He boldly led them against the enemy. As they went forward, they all yelled a very loud and long "Huzzah!"

Major General Wooster was taken off the field by the soldier who first came to his side. He did not know Wooster's back had been broken and that Wooster's wound was mortal. General Wooster, the man who bravely led the charge against the Crown Forces, now lay near death on the field of battle.

Those around Wooster reloaded and fired at the Crown Forces as long as they could. When they saw the bayonet charge drawing near they withdrew. Some stopped every few yards and fired at the advancing force.

Wooster was taken to Danbury. A few days after the battle his family saw him one last time. He died from his wounds at the Dibble House in Danbury.

Wooster's last words were, "I am dying but with a strong hope and persuasion that my country will gain her independence."

Monument to General Daniel Wooster
The tallest monument in the cemetery.
Wooster Cemetery, Danbury, Connecticut.

Wooster Monument Base
This side of the monument depicts Wooster shot in battle.
Wooster Cemetery, Danbury, Connecticut.
Photographs by Larry A. Maxwell, 2017

Larry A. Maxwell

 **Chapter 34**

Sybil Returns Home
April 27, 1777 – About 10 a.m. Sunday

It was about ten o'clock Sunday morning on April 27, 1777. Colonel Henry Ludington left a few hours earlier with about two hundred men,. They headed for Danbury, Connecticut, to help drive back the Crown Forces. On the way they received word the Crown Forces were headed to Ridgefield. They were ordered to proceed there.

The Minute-Men of the Revolution
Lithograph by Currier & Ives, 1876

After the Colonel left, others continued to come in response to Sybil's call on her all-night ride.

Lieutenant Colonel Reuben Ferris and Captain John Crane stayed behind waiting for the rest of the men.

About two hundred more men arrived over the next few hours. They gathered in small clusters. Some started some small campfires to warm themselves.

Jesse Ganong, Sybil's friend, was one who arrived as part of the second group. His father did not want him to go, but he still came.

Jesse was outside the Ludington's house talking with Rebecca, Sybil's younger sister. As they were talking they looked up and saw Sybil returning.

Sybil Ludington's Ride Ends

A historic monument was placed at this site on Route 52, in Kent by the New York State Department of Education in 1932. This was where the Ludington home stood. This is where Sybil ended her ride. That marker was damaged and then replaced in 2008.
Photograph by Larry A. Maxwell, 2018

Sybil came slowly riding up the road toward the house. She was slumped over her horse.

She raised her head as she saw the house. She did not know where she was. She weakly said, "To arms! To arms!"

Jesse and Rebecca ran quickly to Sybil. Rebecca held the bridle as Jesse helped Sybil off her horse.

Rebecca was alarmed to see how tired Sybil looked. As Jesse helped Sybil, Rebecca was so concerned all she could say was, "Sybil!"

Sybil raised her head and attempted to yell one more time, "To arms! To arms!"

She then collapsed in Jesse's arms.

When Sybil's mother, Abigail, saw Sybil ride up she ran to her as fast as she could

When she saw how Sybil looked, she cried out, "Sybil!"

Sybil muttered softly one more time, "To arms!"

Jesse safely held Sybil and spoke to her proudly, "You did it Sybil! You did it!"

Abigail was sad to see Sybil so tired out. But was relieved to see her daughter home safe. With motherly love, Abigail said, "Oh, Sybil! My dear child!"

She told Jesse, "Jesse please take her in the house!"

Jesse was already taking Sybil to the house, yet politely replied, "Yes, Ma'am!"

Jesse, Abigail, and Rebecca went into the house together and took Sybil up to her bed.

Colonial Militia Assemble

Reenactors from the B.A.R. portraying Colonial Militia.
Living History Guild Archival Photograph

Back outside Captain John Crane came to Lieutenant Colonel Reuben Ferris. He took off his hat in salute and respectfully said, "Lieutenant Colonel Ferris."

Ferris tipped the brim and said, "Yes, Captain Crane?"

Crane gave Ferris the word that the men were ready. He said, "Sir, I believe most of the men are here now."

This was the moment they were waiting for. Ferris gave Crane the command, "Have them fall in!"

Crane yelled out the order, "Fall in!"

The men quickly formed orderly rows with their muskets on their left shoulders.

When they were lined up Captain Crane yelled, "Order arms!"

The men quickly came to the *Order Arms* position.

Ferris spoke to the men.

As he was speaking Jesse came back outside. He carried a musket Sybil's mother gave him. He ran and joined the other soldiers in line.

"I am thankful all of you came in response to Sybil's call," Ferris said.

One of the men shouted out, "Three cheers for Sybil!"

All the men took off their hats. They waved them in the air as they shouted three *Huzzahs*!

"Huzzah! Huzzah! Huzzah!"

After the cheer Ferris continued, "As you know by now the British Regulars and their despicable Tory allies raided and burned Danbury last night."

The men responded shouting *Boos* of disapproval.

One of the men man yelled, "Cowards!"

Ferris then updated his men. "Another messenger arrived and said General Benedict Arnold, General Wooster and General Silliman are at Bethel and plan to attack the Crown Forces this morning and drive them back to the sea."

He did not know the Crown Forces left Danbury a few hours ago and were on their way to Ridgefield. A messenger would bring him that news later.

Ferris continued, "I am sure all of you know Colonel Ludington and the first group of men left a few hours ago. We knew many of you had quite a distance to come so Captain Crane and I waited here for the rest of you to arrive."

He knew everyone was tired and he was glad they all came. He continued, "I know you have come a long way, but it is now our time to go join the fight and drive the Redcoats and those blasted Tories into the sea!"

He paused. Then he asked the men, "Are you ready to go join the fight!"

All the men took off their hats. They waved them wildly shouting, "Huzzah! Huzzah! Huzzah!"

Ferris shouted out, "For liberty!"

The men raised their hats again and yelled in response, "For liberty!"

Ferris then ordered them to mount their horses and wagons and head off to join the fight.

Militia at the 225th Anniversary of Sybil's Ride

Reenactors in historically accurate uniforms.
[Left to Right] George Warnecke in Continental Uniform. Others as Militia: Larry A. Maxwell, Nicholas Finelli, Jack Klix, Fred Lambert, Phillip Weaver, and George Bock.
Photograph Carmel, New York, April 2002

Chapter 35

Barricades in Ridgefield
April 27, 1777 – Late Sunday Morning

It was late Sunday morning on April 27, 1777. The people in Ridgefield learned how the Crown Forces invaded Danbury. They hoped and prayed the Crown Forces would go back to their ships the same way they came.

Their hopes were dashed when a messenger arrived in Ridgefield and informed them the force of close to two thousand Crown Forces were on their way back to Norwalk, right through their town.

Captain Ebenezer Jones called the Ridgefield Militia to assemble. He decided to build a barricade in the middle of the road. He picked a spot in town where there were buildings on the west side of the road and a steep drop-off on the east side. A barricade at the spot would provide a good be a good place to slow down the Crown Forces and defend the town.

He called everyone in town to help. Men, women, and children, from all over town came. They brought carts and barrels and chairs and whatever else they could find. They worked together to build the barricade.

Captain Samuel Lawrence arrived with his men from the nearby 3rd Westchester County Militia. They joined in the task of building the barricade.

Barricade at Ridgefield

Barricades erected to block the Crown Forces advance.
Connecticut Historical Society Collection

While the people were building the barricade, General David Wooster launched a series of unexpected attacks north of town, on the Crown Forces.

Those attacks by Wooster and his men slowed down the advance of the Crown Forces. That gained additional time for those in Ridgefield to prepare.

About an hour-and-a-half-ago Colonel Philip Burr Bradley and some fifty men from the 5th Connecticut Regiment of the Continental Line arrived. Many of them were from Ridgefield.

Captain Jones, who was the leader of the Local

Militia, had every right to keep control of the operation. Yet, he turned command over to Colonel Bradley. Bradley was a senior officer in the Continental Army. That one decision changed the direction for the rest of the operation.

The first thing Bradley did was send sentries north to keep watch on the main road leading into town.

He told them, "Go north of town and keep watch for the Crown Forces. As soon as you see them come back and let me know."

The sentries quickly ran up the road.

Bradley had the rest of his men help strengthen the barricade. He walked up and down and carefully inspected the barricade to make sure it was strong.

When he discovered a weak point in the barricade he yelled, "Fill in this gap over here!"

People found more things to help make that part of the barricade stronger.

Everyone was encouraged when close to noon more help arrived. It was General Benedict Arnold and General Silliman. They were on horseback, accompanied by a few hundred Militia.

Colonel Bradley was very glad to see the new arrivals. He stopped to greet them with a very respectful hats-off salute, "General Arnold! General Silliman! It is so good to see you!"

Arnold and Silliman remained on their horses and returned the salute with a proper tip of their hats.

Arnold praised Bradley and his men, "Colonel Bradley,

I see you and your boys from the 5th Connecticut have been busy!"

Bradley said, "Yes, we have."

Bradley gave credit where credit was due. "Captain Ebenezer Jones of the 1st Ridgefield Militia came up with the idea of building this barricade and picked this advantageous spot."

General Arnold looked around as Bradley spoke and saw it was indeed a very good location for the barricade.

Bradley continued, "Captain Samuel Lawrence and the 3rd Westchester County Militia arrived next and helped. When I arrived with my men we joined them. We plan to stop the Crown Forces right here in Ridgefield! They will get no further!"

Arnold was inspired by Bradley's words and dedication and with the work of his men. He respectfully said, "Colonel Bradley it will be an honor for us to stand with you!"

Bradley appreciated Arnold's compliment. He said, "General Arnold, General Silliman, the honor is all ours!"

General Silliman was a general in the Connecticut State Militia. Colonel Bradley, like General Arnold, was an officer in the Continental Line. The fact that Bradley, a Continental Line officer was in charge, meant General Arnold was now the highest-ranking officer present.

Colonel Bradley took off his hat and bowed his head as he said, "General Arnold, you being the senior officer, I respectfully yield command to you and am your humble servant."

Anyone who knew Arnold, knew he liked being in

charge. Up until that point he did not have a problem following to the Connecticut Militia Generals because that was proper military protocol. Yet now that his opportunity to lead arrived. He gladly seized the moment.

Trying not to look to happy, Arnold replied to Bradley, "Colonel Bradley I am honored."

Arnold then got a bold look on his face. He pulled out his sword. He turned his horse around to face the men. Then he clearly and very loudly yelled each word, so all could hear him, "When the Crown Forces come, we will give them lead!"

His words were few but inspired everyone.

All the soldiers, along with General Bradley and General Silliman took off their hats. They waved them in the air and yelled three *Huzzahs*, as Arnold kept his sword raised.

North of town, the Crown Forces finished fighting back the last attack by General Wooster. They pulled their cannon back in line on the muddy road. Then they continued their march south toward Ridgefield.

General Tryon felt victorious and bold. He felt like they could not be beaten. He wanted to let everyone know the Crown Forces were coming. He told his musicians to play as they marched forward.

Chapter 36

Battle in Ridgefield

April 27, 1777 – Early Sunday Afternoon

It was early afternoon on Sunday, April 27, 1777. The Militia and Continental soldiers were working all morning building a barricade in Ridgefield. They hoped to stop the Crown Forces. When the barricade was finished it was filled with two rows of men. They were ready to alternate shooting when the attack began.

Battle of Ridgefield

A Skirmish in America between the Kings Troops & Gen. Arnold.
1780 Engraving published in London by R. Sayer and J. Benet.

Suddenly the people in town heard the sound of the Crown Forces drums and fifes playing military music.

The sentries, sent out earlier, ran down the street in advance of the Crown Forces. It became very clear the enemy was coming down the road toward them and would be there shortly.

Battle of Ridgefield Historic Marker
This marker is located on the main street in Ridgefield, Connecticut, where the main battle started.
Photograph by Larry A. Maxwell, 2017

The sentries climbed over the barricade. Colonel Philip Burr Bradley stood bravely, staring up the road.

General Arnold and General Silliman were on horseback about thirty yards behind the barricade. Their men were ready to stop the Crown Forces if they broke through or went around the barricade.

When Colonel Bradley finally saw the Crown Forces he yelled, "Here they come! "Make ready!"

He waited for the Crown Forces to get closer. Then he shouted, "Present!"

The men pointed their muskets through the barricade. Bradley waited until the Crown Forces to come closer. Then he yelled as loud as he could, "Fire!"

On his command all the soldiers fired their muskets. It sounded like roaring thunder and made the ground shake. Some of the soldiers in the front row of the Crown Forces were hit and fell to the ground.

As soon as the men in the first row behind the barricade fired, they stepped back and let the second row of men step forward to take their place.

The Crown Forces stopped about fifty yards from the barricade. They quickly returned fire with a massive volley. Musket balls ripped through the barricades striking some of Bradley's men with deadly force.

The first row of men who dropped back, reloaded. Bradley gave orders to the second row, who were now at the front of the barricade. This time he gave the commands more rapidly, "Make Ready! Present! Fire!"

Bradley's men fired. As soon as they fired, the Crown Forces returned fire.

Musket fire went back and forth between the Rebels and the Crown Forces. This continued until three British cannon crews brought their guns to the front line.

British Regulars and Loyalists formed lines on each

side of the cannons.

While the cannon crews were loading, the Regulars fired a volley. A few moments later the Loyalists fired.

Bradley yelled to his men, "Fire at will!"

Bradley's men reloaded and returned fire. They each shot their muskets one after another.

Cannon Crew Fires

*Franklyn Maxwell and Xavier Ojeda,
Living History Guild members fire cannon.*
Living History Photograph

Suddenly all three cannons fired. A section of the barricade was blown away, throwing debris and men in different directions.

Bradley called to his men, "Retreat!"

He led his men back from the barricade. As they retreated, some stopped. They turned around, shot back at the enemy, then quickly rejoined the retreat.

The Crown Forces came down the street like a massive wave. They poured through the barricade.

They formed rows and fired at the Rebels. Governor William Tryon and General William Erskine followed their men through the barricade.

Tryon shouted out, sounding more desperate than victorious, "We have broken through and have them on the run! We must advance to the ships!"

General Erskine was concerned at the resistance they faced. He asked Tryon, "What about the goods we captured in Danbury? They are slowing us down."

Tryon yelled, "We must advance swiftly. Have the men take what they can but leave the rest behind! We struck a major blow against these Rebels!"

Erskine yelled to his men, "Take what you can and leave behind whatever slows you down!"

Some soldiers, who were pulling heavy loaded carts, threw aside some of the supplies. Then they moved more quickly through the barricade.

The cannons came forward and fired upon the retreating Rebels. One cannon ball stuck the Keeler Tavern where some of the Rebels took a stand.

Erskine waved his sword and urged his men forward. He yelled, "It is time to return to New York in victory!"

Bradley's men were slowly doing a fighting retreat. They would retreat a little, then stop and shoot back at the Crown Forces. Then they retreated a little further and repeated the process again and again.

General Arnold rode forward leading a large group of

men. He waved his sword and yelled, "Lads! Listen here! We must hold this line! Right here! Right now! For liberty!"

Cannonball in Keeler Tavern
Ridgefield, Connecticut.
Photograph by Larry A. Maxwell - 2018

The men who were retreating stopped and joined Arnold. They formed a line and fired back at the Crown Forces.

A British officer at the head of the Crown Forces came closer. He yelled the command, "Form a Line!"

The Crown Forces stopped and formed two rows more ragged than usual. The officer yelled pausing briefly between each command, "Make Ready! Present! Fire!"

The Crown Forces fired. Arnold and his horse were both hit. His horse was struck by nine musket balls. It fell and pinned him to the ground.

A Connecticut soldier saw Arnold fall and yelled, "They killed General Arnold!"

The Rebel troops scattered and the Crown Forces boldly advanced.

Exploit of Benedict Arnold
Engraving by Kendrick and P. Neeber.
The Youths' History of the United States, 1887

Arnold was pinned under his horse. He struggled to free himself. A Loyalist in a green coat approached him with a bayonet fixed to his musket. He looked at Arnold and yelled, "Surrender! You are my prisoner!"

Arnold pulled his revolver out from his saddle holster and shouted at the Loyalist, "Not yet!"

He then pulled the trigger. The Loyalist's plan to capture Arnold failed as the bullet from Arnold's musket struck him at close range. He fell backwards, and his musket flew out of his hand.

Arnold struggled and freed himself. He picked up his sword and stumbled off to the side.

He saw his men retreating. He gathered his strength and hobbled quickly back to the street. He bravely held his sword high in the air and yelled, "Rally men! Rally!"

The soldier who previously cried, *Arnold is dead*, recognized Arnold's voice. He turned around and yelled, "General Arnold is alive!"

Arnold cried out louder, "Rally around me!"

The men were inspired when they saw and heard General Arnold, who they thought was dead, standing bravely against the enemy. They ran to where he stood and took a stand with him. They fired against the mighty sea of Crown Forces coming toward them.

Soon, General Silliman and his men came forward and reinforced General Arnold and his men. They stood firm refusing to give up the ground to the Crown Forces.

The Crown Forces realized the best thing to do was to go around the Rebels, rather than continue a deadly head-to-head attack. That decision saved many lives.

Chapter 37

Crown Forces South of Ridgefield
April 27, 1777 – Sunday Sunset

It was late Sunday afternoon on April 27, 1777. The sun was about to set. The Crown Forces retreat from Ridgefield was slowed by Rebel Forces pursuing them.

Rebel Militia from surrounding areas poured in all day and joined the attack on the Crown Forces.

Soldiers Return Fire Under Cover
Franklyn Maxwell and Daniel Maxwell, Living History Guild.
Photograph by Larry Maxwell

This brought back bad memories to the men in the Crown Forces from the 4th Regiment of Foot and 23rd Regiment of Foot. It reminded them of how their companions were picked off, two years ago, on their return to Boston after they attacked Lexington and Concord.

Continentals Attack from Woods

John and Kyle Esposito,
Reenactors from 4th N.Y. Regiment.
Living History Guild Photograph

The Crown Forces were now south of Ridgefield near the border of Wilton. It was two days since they landed. Most of them had not slept. Soon it was going to be dark. They were tired and had little strength to go any further.

General William Erskine and his men were near the back of the line of the Crown Forces. They were covering the retreat. All along the way they were followed by

Rebels who fired upon them and then ran away.

As it grew darker the attacks grew less.

They thought the fighting was done for the day. Suddenly they heard the blast of a musket come from the woods. One of the men in line was struck and fell.

Crown Forces Fall to Militia Attack from Woods
Lantern Slide from Story of the Revolution.
New York Public Library Image Collection

Erskine and his men stopped, firmly held their muskets, and looked in the direction of the sound.

A sergeant quickly called to the men near him, "Form two rows, on me!"

They quickly formed two rows, facing the woods.

The sergeant then yelled, "Front row, take a knee!"

The men in the front row got down on one knee. The others stood behind them. Both rows pointed their muskets towards the woods.

The sergeant shouted the command, "Make ready!

Front row! Fire!"

The men in the front fired. Smoke from their muskets filled the air. As soon as they fired, they quickly reloaded.

As they were reloading, another musket blast came from the woods. The ball from that blast struck the sergeant. He fell to the ground.

The men, who were standing next to him, were shaken. They fired back, then quickly reloaded.

Now both rows were loaded. A corporal took charge. He waited, looking for any movement in the woods.

Erskine and his aide also watched carefully.

They waited and then waited some more. Everything was quiet. Nothing happened.

Finally, when it seemed like it was safe, Erskine gave the command, "Take your ease Lads!"

The men breathed a sigh of relief then they lowered their muskets. Those who were kneeling stood.

Erskine then said, "Fall back in line and keep a watch as we move forward."

They started to move forward again. All the while they looked carefully to their left and right. Every few steps the men in the back stopped, turned around and looked, keeping an eye out for a rear attack.

One of Governor Tryon's aides rode up to Erskine. The aide took off his hat in salute and nodded his head. He said, "General Erskine?"

Erskine returned the salute, grabbing the tip of his hat and nodding slightly.

Tryon's aide said, "Governor Tryon requests you to

join him."

Erskine turned to his aide. He said, "Take over."

Erskine's aide nodded his head and replied, "Yes, Sir!"

Erskine then rode off with Tryon's aide.

When Erskine reached Tyron, he gave an informal salute by nodding his head to Governor Tryon. He then said, "Governor Tryon your aide said you wanted to see me?"

Tryon replied, "Yes, General Erskine. The scouts tell me it is still about ten miles to the ships. That is almost half a day's march without any unforeseen delays."

Erskine was very disappointed to hear that. He was hoping they were closer than that. He said, "I did not realize we still had that far to go."

Tryon was frustrated by all the delays and resistance. He said, "We should have reached the ships by now!"

Erskine replied, "Those blasted Rebels have relentlessly been coming up behind us and shooting mercilessly at our men! They fight like dogs! And that has slowed us down significantly. We had no choice but to stop and take a stand every few hundred yards to repel them."

Tryon agreed with Erskine, "That is a good analogy, General Erskine! Those Rebels are like a pack of dogs!"

Though he was greatly disappointed at the way things went, Tryon appreciated how Erskine and his men fought. He spoke words of encouragement. "You and your men have done quite well and fought with honor."

Erskine nodded his head in appreciation of the

compliment, "Thank you Governor."

Tryon then explained, "I believe ten more miles is too far for our men to go. They have not slept in two days and though many have fought valiantly and would march on, if we commanded them. I believe we must stop here, and rest for the night."

Erskine agreed, "I greatly desire to continue on to the ships, but I agree with you, though the spirit is willing, the flesh is indeed weak."

Tryon asked, "Do you think those blasted Rebels will stop pursuing us and take a rest, if we stop?"

Erskine gave that question some thought. Back then very few battles took place in the dark.

He then responded, "Though they are a bunch of dogs, even dogs get tired and need to rest."

Tryon smiled at that reply. He said, "Then set out sentries and tell the men to stop and rest for the night."

Erskine replied, "I am sure they will appreciate that."

The Crown Forces gratefully stopped their retreat and welcomed a chance to get some much-needed rest.

Chapter 38

Ludington Meets Arnold
April 27, 1777 – Late Sunday Evening

Right after the sun set on Sunday, April 27, 1777, General Benedict Arnold was pleased when he learned the Crown Forces stopped to rest for the night south of Ridgefield near the Wilton border. He knew his men were tired and could not fight well in the dark, so he ordered them to rest.

While his men rested Arnold rode south around the Crown Forces to find a good place where his army could take a stand in the morning and inflict the most damage.

Meanwhile Colonel John Lamb and his Continental Artillery, who responded to Silliman's call, arrived near Comp Beach. General Arnold was able to meet with Lamb. They found an ideal place to put the cannon and men to launch an attack. It was near the bridge over the Saugatuck River. That was not far from where the Crown Forces docked their ships.

Lamb put his men in place. Then he returned with Arnold. When they reached the others, Arnold gathered the other officers to discuss plans for the next day.

Larry A. Maxwell

Continental Artillery Fire Cannon

*Artillery attached to the 4th N.Y. Regiment.
Franklyn Maxwell, Doug McKinnon (Lamb's Artillery),
Eric Fiocco and Caleb Arena.*
Photograph by Al Pochek, 2018

A couple of hours earlier, Colonel Henry Ludington and his men arrived in Ridgefield after the battle. They were sad when they saw the destroyed barricade and the dead and wounded scattered around the town.

They were inspired when they learned of General Arnold's brave stand and how the other Militia and Continentals pursued the retreating Crown Forces.

Colonel Ludington and his men did not stay long in Ridgefield. Some tows people gave them food. Then they continued south to join the others to help drive the Crown Forces back to the sea.

It was after nightfall when Colonel Ludington and his men arrived at the place where the Continentals and Militia stopped to rest for the night.

They looked around and saw men huddled around

small campfires warming themselves. Their faces were partially blackened from the blast of their muskets. Many were sleeping after a long hard day.

After their long journey the idea of getting some rest was very appealing to the Colonel and his men.

Off in the distance they could see the campfires from the Crown Forces. That gave them an eerie feeling knowing the enemy was resting so close to them.

Colonel Ludington found a place for his men to rest. They were ready and eager to fight but it looked like the fighting was done for the day and they would be resting for the night. Most of them were extremely tired after traveling all night and day. They welcomed the chance to get some much-needed rest.

The Colonel asked a sentry, "Where are the officers?"

The sentry pointed him in the right direction. The officers were meeting close to where he arrived.

One of the aides standing guard greeted the Colonel, "Sir, may I be of assistance to you?"

Colonel Ludington replied, "Yes, you may young man. I am Colonel Henry Ludington of the 7th Regiment of the Dutchess County Militia. I just arrived from Fredericksburg, New York and am reporting for duty with two hundred men and expect another two hundred men to arrive in a few hours."

When the aide learned Ludington was a colonel, he took off his hat, and nodded his head in a salute. He said, "It is an honor to meet you Colonel Ludington."

He then introduced himself, "My name is Edmond

Ogden with the 5th Connecticut Regiment."

Ogden realized the Colonel and his men travelled quite a distance. He said, "I believe Fredericksburg is more than thirty miles away from here. Is that correct?"

"Yes, it is," Colonel Ludington replied. "I received a message about nine o'clock last night that the Crown Forces invaded and burned Danbury. I sent out my daughter Sybil to ride some forty miles to call out the Militia. When the first two hundred men responded I left my second in command behind to wait for the rest of the men and we came as quickly as we could. We stopped briefly at Ridgefield then proceeded here. The whole trip was about thirty-five miles"

Ogden was amazed at what he just heard. "Let me see if I understand you correctly. You received the message from Danbury about nine o'clock, last night."

"Yes," Colonel Ludington replied.

Ogden asked, "Then you sent out your daughter Cecil to ride some forty miles to call out the Militia?"

"Yes, my daughter rode some forty miles to call out the Militia, but her name is Sybil," he replied.

"Why did you send your daughter, Sybil?" Ogden asked.

Colonel Ludington replied, "Because she is my oldest and she is the best rider I know."

Ogden remembered last night's bad weather. He asked, "And she did that last night when it was raining and cold and dark?"

"That is correct," the Colonel replied.

Ogden wanted to make sure he understood correctly, "If I understand you correctly, your daughter rode forty miles to call out the Militia. That means some of your men had to travel many miles from their homes to your assembly point and then travelled an additional thirty miles with you to get here?"

"Correct again," Colonel Ludington said.

Ogden smiled, "Your daughter must be quite a special young lady. I would love to meet her one day."

He added, "You and your men must be very dedicated, and extremely tired after coming all that distance."

"We are tired, that is true. But we are ready to help drive the Crown Forces back into the sea," Colonel Ludington replied.

Ogden realized he should stop asking questions and introduce the Colonel to the other officers, "Let me introduce you to the other officers. I am sure they will be glad to meet you."

Ogden led Colonel Ludington to the other officers. "Begging you pardon, General Arnold," Ogden said. "I have someone to introduce."

The other officers stopped talking. They looked at Ogden and Colonel Ludington.

General Arnold said, "You may proceed."

Ogden began to introduce the Colonel, "General Benedict Arnold, may I introduce Colonel Henry Ludington of the 7th Regiment of the Dutchess County Militia. He just arrived from Fredericksburg, New York with two hundred reinforcements."

He paused, then said, "He anticipates an additional two hundred more men arriving in a few hours."

General Arnold gladly greeted Colonel Ludington, "Colonel Ludington it is a pleasure to meet you. Your arrival is well timed. We desperately need more men to strike another blow at the Crown Forces."

Ludington took off his hat and bowed his head in a salute. "Thank you, General Arnold, your reputation precedes you. It is an honor to meet you. I am your humble servant."

General Arnold made the rest of the introductions. Each officer nodded his head as he was introduced. "This is General Gold Selleck Silliman of the Connecticut State Militia, Colonel John Burr Bradly of the 5th Connecticut Regiment. And this is Colonel John Lamb of the Continental Artillery. He and his men going to help us teach the Crown Forces a lesson."

Colonel Lamb smiled. He reached out his hand and shook Colonel Ludington's hand. He was one of the leaders of the Sons of Liberty in New York. When the revolution started, he formed his artillery regiment.

Colonel Lamb asked, "Did that soldier say you were from Fredericksburg, New York?"

Ludington replied, "Yes Sir, Colonel Lamb."

Colonel Lamb was familiar with the area. He realized Colonel Ludington and his men came quite a distance. He asked, "Colonel that is a long distance away. How did you and your men arrive as quickly as you did?"

Portrait of Colonel John Lamb

By Benson John Lossing, 1850
Lamb's face was disfigured from a wound he received at the Battle of Quebec. This picture has Lamb's alleged personal signature.
Pictorial Field Book of the Revolution

Ludington replied with a brief summary, "When a messenger arrived from Danbury, my daughter Sybil set out on horseback riding some forty miles to issue the call to arms. As soon as half of our men arrived, I took that first group and we came on horseback and in wagons, so we could get here as quickly as we could."

Lamb complimented him, "Coming on horseback and wagons was a wise move to get here sooner."

Lamb then asked, "Did you say your daughter rode some forty miles to summon the troops?"

Ludington replied proudly, "Yes Sir! She did!"

Arnold was impressed. He complimented Sybil, "Colonel Ludington you have quite a remarkable daughter."

Edmond Ogden spoke up, "Begging the General's pardon, may I add something?"

Arnold replied, "Yes?"

Ogden added, "I thought the General might like to know that after Colonel Ludington's men travelled many miles to the Colonel's house, they went another thirty-five miles all day and night to arrive here, only stopping briefly in Ridgefield."

Arnold was amazed and pleased, He said, "I can see you and your people are very dedicated to the cause."

Ludington humbly replied, "We try to do our best."

Arnold was pleased with that response. He replied, "Your best is all we can ask for."

Arnold then motioned to Colonel Ludington and said., "Come look at what we have planned."

He showed the Colonel the plans for the next day's battle.

Chapter 39

Back at the Ludington's Home
April 28, 1777 – Monday Morning

It was the morning of Monday, April 28, 1777, at the home of Colonel Ludington in Fredericksburg, New York. While the Crown Forces and Rebels were about to enter battle in Norwalk, Sybil Ludington was about forty miles away sleeping safely in her bed.

Abigail, Sybil's mother, entered her room. She came close to Sybil and gently spoke her name, "Sybil."

Sybil was deep in sleep. She was dreaming she was riding to call out the Militia. Suddenly, she sat up yelling, "Call to arms! Call to arms!"

Her Mother reached over, hugged her and said, "It is okay Sybil."

Sybil was startled. She looked around and realized she was only dreaming and was safe at home in her own bed.

When she saw her mother, she said, "I was dreaming."

An excited look came across Sybil's face. She smiled as she said, "I dreamed Father had me ride all night in the cold and rain to call out the Militia."

She looked at her mother and said, "It seemed so real

Mother!"

Abigail smiled and put her arm around Sybil. She reassured her, "It was not a dream. It was real Sybil. You did it!"

The look on Sybil's face changed to one of wonder.

Her mother looked at her and said, "Sybil, I am so proud of you. You rode all night through the rain and through all the dangers and you called out the Militia."

Her mother paused then told her something Sybil did not know. She said, "And they came! Hundreds of them! And they marched off with your father to drive back the Crown Forces!"

Sybil was excited to realize she really did ride and that it made a difference. She was so excited. She said, "Oh Mother!"

Sybil had no idea how long she slept. Her mother decided to let Sybil know, "My dear you slept all day and all through the next night! It is Monday and time to rise and shine and come to breakfast."

Sybil was still in a daze. So many thoughts were going through her mind as she sat on the edge of her bed. She shook her head trying to get oriented.

Her mother smiled then went downstairs.

Sybil rose from her bed. She started to head downstairs but stopped for a moment and looked at herself in the mirror. The girl looking back at her clearly slept very hard.

She said to her image in the mirror, "I am such a mess!"

She quickly brushed her hair. Then she went down the stairs.

When she reached the bottom of the stairs, her sister Rebecca ran over to her. She said, "You did a wonderful job, Sybil!"

Archibald looked up from his place at the table. He said, "I wish I could have done the ride!"

Sybil looked at him with a smile and said, "Perhaps one day you will, Archibald."

Their mother shook her head and smiled.

Henry, Jr., looked at Sybil and said, "So do we call her Sybil Revere now?"

They all laughed.

Abigail then said. "Let us pray for this meal and especially for safety for Father and the others."

Colonial Dining Area

This is similar to the place where Sybil and her family ate. Old Postcard of 1752 Colonial Kitchen.

Chapter 40

British Officers Before Last Battle
April 28, 1777 – Monday Morning

It was early in the morning on Monday, April 28, 1777. The Crown Forces rested overnight south of Ridgefield. They were near the border of Wilton on their way back to their ships which were at Compo Beach near Norwalk.

The Crown Forces did not have any tents because their commanders thought that after they marched to Danbury and captured the Rebel supplies, they would have slept one night in homes in Danbury. They expected to be back in their ships by the following night. It took longer than expected so they had to sleep on the ground. Some slept against trees, some against walls.

That was the first rest many of them had since they landed in at Norwalk more than two days ago.

After rising in the morning, the army marched into Wilton. Some local Loyalists brought them food for breakfast. They made it a short stop. The did not do any looting because they expected the Rebels, who were pursuing them last night, to be reach them at any time.

They did not know the entire Rebel army left early in the morning. They were led by General Benedict Arnold. They marched around the Crown Forces and were now between them and their ships at Compo Beach.

Continental Army and Militia on the March
Soldiers from the Brigade of the American Revolution.
Living History Guild Archival Photograph

Governor William Tryon, General James Agnew, General William Erskine, and General Montfort Browne had a quick breakfast in one of the Loyalist's homes.

Erskine spoke up. "Governor Tryon, thank you for allowing the men to rest last night. I am sure they could not have gone any further without a night's rest."

Browne said, "If it was not for those blasted Rebels we would have been in our ships and on our way back to New York by now!"

Erskine could not contain the disgust he felt for Browne and his Loyalists. Erskine and his men were professional soldiers. In his mind Browne's men were not professionals. They were almost lower than the Rebel Militia. He questioned their loyalty and saw them as people seeking their own gain. His view was strengthened by their conduct which he saw on this raid.

Erskine spoke up, "Were it not for your undisciplined Loyalists getting drunk and acting so improperly in Danbury, and stirring up such an impassioned resistance, we would have been safe back in New York City by now!"

Browne did not like Erskine's previous comments but this time he had enough. He angrily replied, "General Erskine, I have had enough of your disrespect and complaining!"

He stood up and continued speaking boldly, "I would think twice, if I were you, before you speak ill of me or my brave Loyalists! Were it not for those Loyalists fighting faithfully for our King you and your men would have been defeated and would be back in England, long before this!"

Erskine sneered as Browne spoke.

Browne continued, "My men are loyal subjects of King George and they want to stop this Rebellion which was started by their traitorous neighbors who disregard and dishonor our King! My Loyalists have every right to celebrate when they have a victory because of their loyalty to their Crown and country!"

He spoke of the abuse his men experienced at the

hands of their Rebel neighbors, "They had their houses and lands taken away by those infernal Rebels! Many of them have been spit at, mocked, abused, and even imprisoned by those God forsaken Rebels! All because of their loyalty to the Crown!"

As Erskine was thinking about what Browne was saying, the sneer disappeared from his face.

Browne continued, speaking with even greater passion. "Do not criticize them! Let them plunder those who have stolen from them! Let them burn down every Rebel home! And let them do whatever it takes to demoralize and destroy those who would do anything to prolong this Rebellion!"

He reminded the others how well his men just fought, "Look how well my Loyalists fought at Ridgefield! They marched defiantly into Rebel musket fire and drove them back!"

Browne stopped, squared his shoulders and said, "I am proud of my Loyalists! And you should be too!"

His response explained how some of the Loyalists though. It explained why they acted the way they did. That was something Erskine had not considered.

Erskine humbly realized he misjudged Browne and his men. Erskine was a man of character. He took off his hat and bowed apologetically to Browne.

Tryon replied, "That was well put General Browne. I had not considered that before."

Browne was pleased.

Tryon then changed the subject. He said, "It is a good

thing Rebels get tired too. It was a fairly quiet night."

A soldier entered and spoke to Browne.

Browne then updated the others, "My scouts told me Rebel reinforcements and cannon arrived during the night."

Erskine then brought up a sore point, which he learned during the night. "Governor Tryon, I heard your adversary, Colonel Ludington and his Militia arrived during the night."

Tryon showed his disgust for Ludington, "Yes! That blasted Ludington is determined to make my life miserable. I shall have to raise the bounty on his head!"

Browne smiled. Then said, "Or perhaps you shall have his head today!"

Tryon shook his head in agreement with that idea.

Tryon then changed the subject back to the day's plan. "General Erskine, as I lead the troops to the ships, I need you to reinforce the rear lines. I am sure the Rebels will try to hit us with all they have."

Erskine nodded in agreement. He said, "Then we will hit them back!"

Erskine paused. He looked at Browne and proved his change of heart. He said, "And I am sure General Browne and his men will make those Rebels think twice before they oppose those loyal to the King!"

Browne smiled and said, "That we will!"

Browne then said, "Long live the King!"

Tryon and Erskine replied, "Long live the King!"

Chapter 41

Battle in Norwalk
April 28, 1777 – Monday Morning

Early in the morning on Monday, April 28, 1777, before the Crown Forces rose and marched into Wilton, General Benedict Arnold led the American Forces undetected around the Crown Forces, to Norwalk.

Arnold had Colonel John Lamb and his artillery and the Fairfield County Artillery, near the Saugatuck Bridge. They were in a field across from the road which led to Compo Beach, where the Crown Forces fleet was docked.

He placed Colonel Henry Ludington, Captain Edmund Baker, and their men from the 7th Regiment of the Dutchess County Militia along a stone wall, not far from the artillery.

Shortly before the Crown Forces arrived, General Arnold sent Edmond Ogden with an important message, to Colonel Ludington.

When he arrived, he said, "Colonel Henry Ludington, I have a message for you from General Arnold."

The Colonel was waiting to receive his orders. He remembered Ogden. He smiled and said, "Greetings

Edmond Ogden, what word do you have for me?"

Ogden said, "The Crown Forces are drawing near. Colonel Lamb and the artillery will begin the engagement then you are to launch your attack as soon as Colonel Lamb finishes his artillery barrage."

The Colonel said, "Thank you, Edmond, you may return and tell General Arnold I received his orders and will comply."

Ogden replied, "General Arnold said I am to stay with you and report back to him after the action."

The Colonel smiled and patted Ogden on the shoulder. He said, "Then stay you shall!"

Ogden smiled and said, "Yes, Colonel!"

While Colonel Ludington and Ogden were talking, Lieutenant Colonel Reuben Ferris, Captain John Crane, and the rest of Colonel Ludington's Militia arrived. Sybil's friend, Jesse Ganong, was with them.

Ferris had his men stretch their legs. He left Captain Crane in charge as he went to see Colonel Ludington.

He took his hat off in salute and said, "Colonel Ludington, Captain John Crane and I, and the rest of the 7th Regiment of the Dutchess County Militia are reporting for duty."

The Colonel was very happy to see them. He shook Ferris' hand and said, "Reuben, it is so good to see you!"

Ferris said, "Thanks to your daughter Sybil's courageous ride, the rest of the men arrived in the morning some hours after you left. We then set out on our horses and wagons. We stopped very briefly in

Ridgefield and then came here as fast as we could."

Ferris paused and, "It was a very long march and I must admit we are tried."

Then, with a gleam in his eye he added, "But we are ready to fight!"

The Colonel asked the question he had on his mind ever since he left home, "How is Sybil?"

Ferris smiled. He gladly said, "She made it back before we left. She looked exhausted, but she is safe."

Colonel Ludington gave a big sigh of relief, "Thanks be to God!"

The cannons were firing before Ferris arrived. While they were talking the Colonel noticed the firing stopped.

He realized the time for the attack had come. He gave Ferris orders, "You arrived just in time. The artillery barrage has stopped. It is time to attack. Bring your men over here and fall in behind my men."

Ferris ran back to his men and had them fall in. Though they were all very tired they eagerly grabbed their muskets and marched with Ferris over to the Colonel.

Colonel Ludington addressed his men, "This is Edmond Ogden from the 5th Connecticut Regiment. General Arnold sent our orders through him. Our orders are to attack when the cannon barrage stops."

He paused, then continued, "As you can hear the cannon barrage has stopped."

He then spoke with passion, "It is time for us to show the Crown Forces we will not sit idly by and allow them to take away our freedom! We will not put up with injustice! We will make them pay! Follow me and we will drive the Crown Forces into the sea!"

The men yelled, "Huzzah! Huzzah! Huzzah!"

Colonel Ludington called out, "Prime and load!"

The command was echoed down the line.

As soon as the men finished loading the Colonel yelled the command, "First company, advance!"

The soldiers yelled out a loud, "Huzzah!" as the Colonel led the first group over the wall.

Sybil's friend Joseph Angevine was in that group.

When that first group was a few yards away from the wall the Colonel yelled, "Take Care! Halt!"

His men stopped and formed a line.

He yelled, "Make Ready!"

Continental Soldiers Maneuvering in Battle

Men of the 2nd N.Y. and 4th N.Y. Regiments.
Living History Guild Archival Photograph

The men all cocked their muskets.

He then said, "Present!"

They all pointed their muskets at the enemy across the field.

He paused. Then he yelled, "Fire!"

The whole line of men shot their muskets. The sound echoed across the field. A cloud of smoke filled the air.

The Crown Forces, who were coming down the road across the field, formed a line and returned fire.

Colonel Ludington shouted, "Prime and load!"

As they reloaded, the second company under Ferris's command, crossed the wall. They went a few yards past the Colonel and his men.

Ferris yelled, "Take care! Halt!"

They all stopped.

They were already loaded so Ferris gave the orders, "Make Ready! Present! Fire!"

Ferris's men fired.

The Crown Forces fired back.

Some of Ferris' men were hit.

Jesse Ganong was among those struck. He was thrown back and fell to the ground, seriously wounded.

Joseph was alarmed as he saw his friend Jesse fall. He ran over to help him. He could see Jesse was seriously wounded. He did his best to stop the bleeding.

Colonel Ludington, Edmond Ogden, and the others in the first group, went bravely past Ferris' company. They yelled a prolonged, *Huzzah*.

Then they stopped and fired again.

Larry A. Maxwell

As soon as the Colonel's group fired, Ferris and his men went past them and continued the musket fire.

The attack by Colonel Ludington and his men made the Crown Forces stop and take a different route. Muskets continued to fire. The smoke from the muskets filled the field with smoke and made it hard to see.

Patriot's Monument at Compo Beach
Made by H. Daniel Webster. 1910 cast by Tiffany & Co.
Photograph by Larry Maxwell, 2017

Chapter 42

The Smoke Clears
April 28, 1777 - Monday

It was Monday April 28, 1777. The battle which started near Saugatuck Bridge quickly shifted to Compo Beach. As soon as the first part of the Crown Forces were attacked the rest of their force stopped their advance. They turned aside and headed to Compo Beach another way. That decision saved many lives.

General Benedict Arnold quickly sent the artillery and the rest of his force to attack the Crown Forces on Compo Beach.

General William Erskine and his men fought bravely, holding off the Rebels, while the rest of the Crown Forces boarded the ships.

A musket ball passed through General Arnold's coat, but he was not hit. Though he escaped injury he had the horse he was riding was shot.

Colonel John Lamb was not as fortunate. During this battle he left his cannons under the command of one of his men. He then led an attack against the British. He was climbing over a barrier when he was struck down and seriously wounded. He barely survived.

When the battle ended, and the smoke cleared, the surviving Crown Forces were aboard their ships heading back to New York City.

The Battle of Compo Hill by Hannan
Eugene E. Hannan, series of bas relief plaster 1936-1937.
Westport Schools Permanent Art Collection

The Battle of Cedar Point by Hannan
Eugene E. Hannan - 22' long bas relief plaster 1936-1937.
Westport Schools Permanent Art Collection.

After the battle, Colonel Henry Ludington and his men went back to the stone wall where they left their horses and wagons.

They found Joseph Angevine and Jesse Ganong along the wall. Joseph was caring for Jesse, who was badly wounded. He was very bloody and did not look well.

Friend Helping Wounded Soldier
Engraving from Harper's Weekly, June 28, 1858.

Jesse was pale and very weak, yet looked up at the Colonel and asked, "Colonel? Did we win?"

The Colonel said, "Yes, Jesse. Thanks to you we did. We drove them back to the sea like scared rabbits."

Jesse tried to smile. But as he moved in pain, he coughed up some blood.

The Colonel leaned close near Jesse. He said, "Thank you for taking a stand and helping us."

Jesse coughed again. A very concerned look came over his face. He had an important message. He struggled to get out each word, "Colonel ... please ... tell my father ... I am ... sorry."

As soon as Jesse said the last word he passed out and his body went limp. Joseph cried for his friend.

The Colonel took off his hat. He bowed his head and said, "No need to apologize Jesse, no need at all."

Two men came over with a two-wheel cart. They picked up Jesse's body and loaded it in the cart.

The rest of the men got on their horses and in their wagons. They began the long march home.

Everyone was very sad some fell. They were glad to know those did not fall in vain. They knew they took a stand for liberty and caused serious damage on the Crown Forces who dared to invade their land.

After this battle the war continued, yet the Crown Forces never tried another deep inland attack in Connecticut.

ADVERTISEMENT.

LOST, this Summer, in the Enclosures about New York in North America,

The BRITISH ARMY.

Whoever can give an Account of it to his Majesty's Secretary at War, shall not only receive a large Premium, but have the high Honour of killing his Majesty's Hand.—A Part of it is said to have been seen in the Spring near Danbury; but its Stay was so short, that its Tracks were not deep enough to be traced.

Newspaper Advertisement for Lost British Army
The Public Advertiser, August 4, 1777 edition, London.

 **Chapter 43**

The Return
April 30, 1777 - Wednesday

It was Wednesday, April 30, 1777. A lot happened since Sybil Ludington made her courageous all night, forty-mile ride in the rain, to call out the Militia.

Those whose had loved ones respond to the alarm were waiting for word of what happened.

Joseph Angevine's father Jacob was having a cup of tea with Abigail, Sybil, and Rebecca. He came to their house, the night of the alarm. He could not go with the militia. He helped by staying and keeping guard at the Ludington's.

As they were having their tea, Abigail said, "I wonder how much longer it will be until we hear some word?"

Jacob looked at her kindly. He said, "I think we will be hearing something soon."

Sybil said, "I hope they drove the Crown Forces back into the sea!"

Jacob smiled as he said. "I think my son Joseph, would try to do that on his own!"

Sybil had a firm look on her face as she said, "And I

would too!"

Rebecca added, "Me Too!"

There was a knock at the door. Jacob got up, grabbed a musket, and headed to the door. He was followed by Abigail and Sybil. When they opened the door there stood John Ganong. His son Jesse responded to the call.

He humbly asked, "Any word yet?"

After Jesse left to help drive back the Crown Forces, John came to the Ludington's home each day. He was looking to see if there was any word about his son.

As the others stood there, Sybil replied, "No word yet, Mr. Ganong."

John was upset and sad. He said, "I was so wrong! I did not realize they would attack us like that!"

While they were talking, Archibald, one of Sybil's younger brothers, was looking out the window for any sign of his father. Suddenly he got a very happy look on his face. He ran past Jacob, his mother, his sister and Mr. Ganong, shouting, "Mother! Sybil! Everyone! Look! It is Father!"

They looked up the road and saw Colonel Ludington on his horse and a whole group of others coming. They looked tired and very dirty. They marched two days, without much rest, to return home.

His family were thrilled to see him. They all ran to greet him. He got off his horse and ran toward them.

Abigail was so happy. Tears of joy went down her cheeks. She ran and hugged her husband. She joyfully said one word, "Henry!"

Soldiers Return from Battle

Members of the 2nd, 3rd, and 4th New York Regiments.
Living History Guild Archival Photograph

Sybil and her siblings ran to their father and joined their mother hugging him. They yelled, "Father! Father!"

Edmond Ogden had come with the Colonel. He stood back a few paces. He smiled as he watched the happy reunion. Sybil looked at him wondering who he was.

Colonel Ludington said, "Sybil! Thanks to you we arrived at a time when we were able to provide much needed help."

Edmond Ogden added, "And we drove the Redcoats and Tories into the sea!"

Abigail said, "Henry! That is wonderful news!"

Sybil was excited but was also very curious. She looked at Ogden and asked, "Father, who is this?"

Edmond started to reply, "I am ... "

He was interrupted by Sybil's father before he could

get his name out, "This is Edmond Ogden. He is a good man. He served bravely by my side."

She liked what she saw and liked that her father said Edmond was a good and brave man. She gave a curtsey and said, "My name is Sybil, pleased to meet you."

Ogden smiled, gave Sybil a bow and said, "So, Colonel, is this the amazingly brave daughter you were telling me about?"

That made a big smile appear on Sybil's face.

Colonel Ludington looked at Ogden, then looked at his daughters Sybil, Rebecca, and Mary. He wisely replied, "Yes Edmond, that is one of my amazing daughters."

Sybil, Rebecca, and Mary all smiled.

Ogden said, "Colonel, you did not tell me that she is as fair and beautiful as she is brave."

Sybil blushed. Rebecca and Mary giggled.

Ogden then looked at Abigail and said, "I can see she got her charm and good looks from her mother."

Abigail smiled and said, "Why, Henry! It is so nice you brought back such a fine gentleman."

The Colonel smiled and spoke in jest, "Yes, I thought I would bring back a suitable husband for Sybil!"

Abigail was shocked at what Henry said. Then she smiled when she realized he was joking.

Sybil smiled and gave her father a push, as she sternly said, "Father!"

Ogden was surprised. He looked at Henry and said, "Colonel?"

The Colonel realized Ogden did not know he was jesting. He put his hand on Ogden's shoulder and said, "I am just kidding."

Ogden's face showed he liked what he saw in Sybil. She also liked what she saw in him. They liked each other so much, that a few years later they were married.

While Colonel Ludington was having this nice reunion with his family, Jacob Angevine was looking down the line of returning soldiers for his son. John Ganong was also looking for his son.

They finally saw Joseph Angevine pulling a cart. Jacob was happy. He ran over and hugged his son.

John knew Joseph was a friend of his son Jesse. He was very concerned when he saw a body in the cart Joseph was pulling. The body had a hat over its face.

John stopped. He was very upset when he realized the body in the cart was that of his son Jesse. He ran to the cart crying, "Oh no! My son! My son!"

Joseph stopped pulling the cart. He wiped his brow and nodded to John that it was Jesse in the cart.

John threw himself on Jesse crying.

After a few moments John was shocked.

His son Jesse woke up.

When Jesse saw his father he spoke weakly, "Father?"

John's sorrow was replaced by joy. He yelled, "Son! My son! You are alive!"

John tightly hugged Jesse.

Colonel Ludington, Edmond Ogden, Sybil and all the others came over to the cart.

Jesse spoke to his father, "Forgive me, Father! I did not mean to dishonor you!"

John shook his head as he said, "No! Forgive you?? Dishonor me? Oh, No! Son! Will you forgive me! I was an old fool! I had my head buried in the sand! I could not see! I was blinded to the tyranny!"

He paused then said, "But now, now I can finally see! Thanks to you! I know now there is a time to take a stand against tyranny, no matter how hard that may be."

John stopped. He looked at Jesse and said, "Jesse, I am so proud of you!"

Henry put his arm around Abigail and Sybil and said, "Yes! Our children can make us very proud!"

Tombstones of Sybil & Colonel Henry Ludington

Maple Avenue Cemetery, Route 311, Patterson, New York.
Sybil's name is spelled "Sibbell Ludington" on her stone.
Photographs by Larry A. Maxwell, 2017

About the Author
Larry A. Maxwell

Larry A. Maxwell is a historian and author. While working as a journalist he won the coveted Associated Press Writing Award.

He served as Chairman of the Company of Military Historians at West Point.

He is the New York State Town Historian for Patterson, New York. During the Revolutionary War, Patterson was part of Fredericksburg, Dutchess County, New York. Sybil Ludington and her family lived in Fredericksburg.

He has served more than twenty years as Pastor of the *Patterson Baptist Church*. The church was originally called *The Baptist Church of Fredericksburg*. It is the oldest Baptist Church, still in existence, in New York State. The Ludington family donated the property where the church had its first building. Sybil Ludington and Edmond Ogden were married in the church. That church was part of the *Danbury Baptist Association* which wrote a letter to President Thomas Jefferson, to which he responded with his famous *Separation of Church and State* letter.

He is a re-enactor and historical tailor. He is the founder and director of *The Living History Guild*, an organization which helps re-enactors keep history alive. He is also commander of the 4th New York Regiment of the Continental Line.

He served as a historical advisor and costumer for film projects and appeared on screen in numerous productions.

He wrote a companion screenplay for this book. He also wrote another children's book about Sybil Ludington and some of the events in this book. It is called *Travels Through Time – A Revolutionary Adventure*.

He is available to speak at conferences and at historical or educational events or functions. He often speaks wearing historical attire. He also does book signings. He can be contacted at LarryMaxwell@cheerful.com

Larry A. Maxwell

www.ingramcontent.com/pod-product-compliance
Lightning Source LLC
Chambersburg PA
CBHW071305110526
44591CB00010B/782